Incorporation

Made E-Z

MADE E-Z PRODUCTS™ Inc.
Deerfield Beach, Florida / www.MadeE-Z.com

Incorporation Made E-Z™
© Copyright 2000, 2001 Made E-Z Products, Inc.
Printed in the United States of America

 384 South Military Trail
Deerfield Beach, FL 33442

http://www.MadeE-Z.com
All rights reserved.

2 3 4 5 6 7 8 9 1

This publication is designed to provide accurate and authoritative information in regard to subject matter covered. It is sold with the understanding that neither the publisher nor author is engaged in rendering legal, accounting, or other professional services. If legal advice or other expert assistance is required, the services of a competent professional should be sought. From: *A Declaration of Principles jointly adopted by a Committee of the American Bar Association and a Committee of Publishers.*

Incorporation Made E-Z™

Library of Congress Catalog Card Number: 00-092054

Limited warranty and disclaimer

This self-help product is intended to be used by the consumer for his/her own benefit. It may not be reproduced in whole or in part, resold or used for commercial purposes without written permission from the publisher.

This product is designed to provide authoritative and accurate information in regard to the subject matter covered. However, the accuracy of the information is not guaranteed, as laws and regulations may change or be subject to differing interpretations. Consequently, you may be responsible for following alternative procedures, or using material different from those supplied with this product.

Neither the author, publisher, distributor nor retailer are engaged in rendering legal, accounting or other professional services. Accordingly, the publisher, author, distributor and retailer shall have neither liability nor responsibility to any party for any loss or damage caused or alleged to be caused by the use of this product.

Copyright notice

The purchaser of this guide is hereby authorized to reproduce in any form or by any means, electronic or mechanical, including photocopying, all forms and documents contained in this guide, provided it is for non-profit, educational or private use. Such reproduction requires no further permission from the publisher and/or payment of any permission fee.

The reproduction of any form or document in any other publication intended for sale is prohibited without the written permission of the publisher. Publication for non-profit use should provide proper attribution to Made E-Z Products.

Table of contents

How to use this guide

Made E-Z Products™ Guides can help you achieve an important legal objective conveniently, efficiently and economically. But it is important to properly use this guide if you are to avoid later difficulties.

- ◆ Carefully read all information, warnings and disclaimers concerning the legal forms in this guide. If after thorough examination you decide that you have circumstances that are not covered by the forms in this guide, or you do not feel confident about preparing your own documents, consult an attorney.

- ◆ Complete each blank on each legal form. Do not skip over inapplicable blanks or lines intended to be completed. If the blank is inapplicable, mark "N/A" or "None" or use a dash. This shows you have not overlooked the item.

- ◆ Always use pen or type on legal documents—never use pencil.

- ◆ Avoid erasures and "cross-outs" on final documents. Use photocopies of each document as worksheets, or as final copies. All documents submitted to the court must be printed on one side only.

- ◆ Correspondence forms may be reproduced on your own letterhead if you prefer.

- ◆ Whenever legal documents are to be executed by a partnership or corporation, the signatory should designate his or her title.

- ◆ It is important to remember that on legal contracts or agreements between parties all terms and conditions must be clearly stated. Provisions may not be enforceable unless in writing. All parties to the agreement should receive a copy.

- ◆ Instructions contained in this guide are for your benefit and protection, so follow them closely.

- ◆ You will find a glossary of useful terms at the end of this guide. Refer to this glossary if you encounter unfamiliar terms.

- ◆ Always keep legal documents in a safe place and in a location known to your spouse, family, personal representative or attorney.

Introduction to Incorporation Made E-Z™

Millions of Americans choose to incorporate their business each year. Whether you convert your present business or incorporate a startup venture, *Incorporation Made E-Z* guides you through the incorporation process.

Once you have decided that the corporation is the correct form of organization for your business, you must go through the legal steps required to create your corporation. These steps vary from state to state and they also vary in complexity. But with careful planning, you can organize you own corporation—clearly, conveniently, and without costly legal fees.

Using the forms which generally conform to the legal requirements of all states (although it may be necessary to obtain certain state-specific forms from your Secretary of State's office) and information in this guide, you can incorporate in any state without a lawyer, and conduct meetings, record minutes, and protect your personal assets from business debts.

Now anyone can incorporate their business with a minimum of headaches and legal fees—in this guide, we've made it E-Z!

Should you incorporate your business?

1

Chapter 1

Should you incorporate your business?

What you'll find in this chapter:

➡ Choosing the right business entity

➡ The sole proprietorship

➡ The partnership

➡ The limited liability company

➡ When it's right to incorporate your business

Whether to incorporate or to conduct a business in some other form—a sole proprietorship or a partnership, for example—involves many considerations. If you are currently in business, you are busy running the business, which often prevents you from taking time out to carefully consider your options, assess your situation and plan. Even if you are not yet in business but planning to start a new enterprise, do not rush into business without first deciding on the best form of organization. Many factors determine the form and structure of a business enterprise.

Some of the more important considerations in determining what type of business entity is best for your situation include:

- liability and personal exposure

- costs, including filing fees and tax considerations

- the available methods of raising capital

- the ability to attract and keep key personnel through various fringe benefits or participations such as stock options

The four basic forms of business entity are:

1) individual or sole proprietorship

2) partnership

3) limited liability company

4) corporation

Each offers unique advantages and disadvantages.

 note A less complicated and more affordable business structure is generally best for new businesses. As your business grows, you can always change its structure for additional liability protection or tax benefits.

The sole proprietorship

The sole proprietorship is the simplest form of business organization. A sole proprietorship is a business that is owned by an individual who is solely responsible for all aspects of the business. The owner is personally responsible for all debts of the business, even in excess of the amount invested. The business and its owner are thus considered the same entity.

The advantages of a sole proprietorship include:

- low start-up costs, as legal and filing fees are at a minimum. However, many states and cities require a filing with the county clerk, especially if a fictitious business name is adopted. A fictitious name is any name other than the registered name, under which the company does business. A fictitious name is often referred to by the letters DBA (doing business as...)

- greatest freedom from regulation and paperwork

- owner is in direct control, with no interference from other owners

- taxes may be lower than for regular corporations

The disadvantages of a sole proprietorship include:

- unlimited liability. The proprietor is responsible for the full amount of business debts no matter how incurred, which means that his personal property may be taken to cover debts of the business. This, of course, is a significant disadvantage.

- unstable business life, since the sole owner's death or illness would terminate the business

- difficulty in raising capital and in obtaining long-term financing, because an ownership interest in the business cannot readily be sold

The partnership

A partnership is a legal entity that is jointly owned by two or more individuals (although in some cases partners may also be corporations or other entities). As with a sole proprietorship, the owners are personally liable for all debts of the firm unless a special type of partnership, the limited partnership, is set up. Limited partnerships are complex legal structures, and one partner must retain unlimited liability for the debts of the firm. Even partnership agreements for regular partnerships can be quite complex. For more information, see the Made E-Z Products™ guide *Partnerships Made E-Z*.

The advantages of a partnership include:

- low start-up costs, usually with fewer filing fees and franchise taxes

- a broader management base than a sole proprietorship, and a more flexible management structure than a corporation

- possible tax advantages, since it avoids the double taxation of corporation and because income can be taxed at personal income rates. Naturally, the personal income situations of the partners could make this a disadvantage

- the potential for additional sources of capital and leverage by adding limited and special partners

> **note** A comprehensive written partnership agreement is not required by law to form your partnership. However, if you do not have a partnership agreement, then state statutes determine many aspects of your ownership, decision making, dissolution, and winding down rights.

- the duration of the entity can be limited to a stated time, or can continue indefinitely by amendment

The disadvantages of a partnership include:

- unlimited liability of at least one partner and possibly all partners, except in limited partnership situations. The personal assets of the general partners are available to satisfy partnership debts

> **note** Consider the problems and disputes that could potentially develop: disputes between partners; a partner who leaves, dies or becomes incapacitated; a partner who takes a partnership opportunity for himself or herself; a partner who causes harm to the partnership.

- the life of a partnership is unstable, since changing partners by adding new ones or by death or departure of partners causes the partnership to terminate

- obtaining large sums of capital is relatively difficult, as financing cannot be obtained from the public through a stock offering

- the acts of just one partner, even unauthorized acts in many cases, bind all partners

- an individual partnership interest cannot be sold or transferred easily

- most tax-supported fringe benefits, such as pension and profit-sharing arrangements available to corporations, are unavailable to partnerships

The limited liability company

A limited liability company is a business entity created by legislation. It combines the advantages of a corporation with those of a partnership. This type of company is similar to a corporation in that it offers limited personal liability to its owners. It is similar to a partnership in that it offers the partnership's tax advantages to its owners. Therefore, forming a limited liability company provides management with a great deal of organizational flexibility.

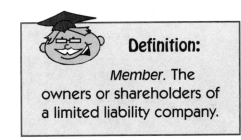

Definition:

Member. The owners or shareholders of a limited liability company.

The advantages of a limited liability company include:

- double taxation is avoided. Since it is not a corporation, there is no corporate income tax. Income is based on the personal level, as in a partnership.

- personal liability is limited. All personal assets of the partners are protected from corporate creditors. Managers and officers are also protected if they participate in the operation of the company.

- there is relatively little paperwork and recordkeeping beyond a simple operating agreement or statement of the principles of the organization

- you can form a limited liability company yourself. The forms are available from the secretary of state of the state in which you want to form the company. You do not need an attorney. For helpful information about forming your own LLC, see Made E-Z Product's *Limited Liability Companies Made E-Z.*

- you can convert your present corporation to a limited liability company and begin receiving the benefits immediately

Definition:
Articles of Organization. The records needed to be filed to establish an LLC, similar to Articles of Incorporation.

- it is relatively inexpensive to establish a limited liability company, usually costing less than $500 to register with the state

- annual registration fees are low, under $250 in most states

The disadvantages of a limited liability company include:

- although every state now recognizes the limited liability company, there is still a lack of widespread public acceptance, because this type of company is relatively new. Limited liability companies have only been recognized by the IRS since 1988.

- multi-state businesses may have tax problems if they conduct business in states that recognize limited liability companies and in states that do not

- IRS rules governing insolvency may create problems for the owners of the limited liability company

Definition:
Operating Agreement. The rules adopted that spell out the company's operating procedures. Similar to a corporation's by-laws.

- limited liability companies do not enjoy the advantages of IRS rulings when there is a sale of worthless stock or stock sold at a loss

- the sale of 50 percent or more of the ownership of the limited liability company in any 12-month period ends any tax advantages the company may have had with the IRS

- limited liability companies may not engage in tax-free reorganizations

As the public, accountants and financial planners become more familiar with the limited liability company, the popularity of this form of business organization is expected to grow.

The corporation

A corporation is a business that is formed and authorized by law to act as a single entity, although it may be owned by one or more persons. It is legally endowed with rights and responsibilities and has a life of its own independent of the owners and operators. It has been defined by the United States Supreme Court as "an artificial being, invisible, intangible and existing only in contemplation of the law." To fully understand the

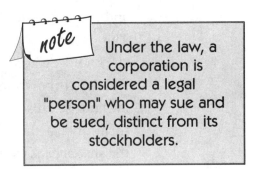

note Under the law, a corporation is considered a legal "person" who may sue and be sued, distinct from its stockholders.

concept of a corporation, you must think of it as a distinct and independent entity and one separate from its owners.

The advantages of a corporation include:

- Limited liability. The owners are not personally liable for debts and obligations of the corporation. They can personally lose only to the extent of their investment in the corporation, with the exception that they can be personally liable for certain types of taxes, such as payroll taxes withheld from the employees' paychecks but not paid to the IRS and state tax authorities. If the business fails or loses a lawsuit, the general creditors cannot attach the owners' homes, cars and other personal property. Limited liability is the one major reason so many businesses are incorporated.

- Capital can be raised more easily than under other forms of ownership. This does not mean, however, that a new corporation can sell shares of stock easily. The sale of stock is highly regulated by both federal and state governments, and obtaining bank loans for a fledgling business may be no easier for a new corporation than for a partnership or proprietorship.

- Ownership in a corporation is more easily transferable; this includes transferring shares to family members as gifts or otherwise, as well as selling your interest to some other person. However, in many small corporations it is advisable to put restrictions on transfer of shares, especially if the persons owning and working in the business must be able to work closely together. This is generally accomplished by stockholder agreements. The stockholder's agreement is an agreement between a shareholder and the corporation. It may state, for example, that the shareholder may not sell his shares for a specific period of time after acquiring them or that the shareholder must, under certain conditions, sell the shares back to the corporation.

- Since the corporation is an independent legal entity, it has a life of its own, or a continuous existence. It does not cease simply because one of the owners dies or wishes to retire.

- A corporation has a defined, centralized management. Control rests in the board of directors, whose powers are exercised through the officers.

- Many companies offer discounts (in areas like travel) to corporations.

- Retirement funds, defined-contribution plans, money-purchase plans and other profit-sharing, pension and stock-option plans may be more easily set up with a corporation.

The disadvantages of a corporation include:

- Corporations are subject to more governmental regulations than either partnerships or sole proprietorships.

- Corporations are among the most expensive form of business to organize, although a partnership may be equally expensive.

- There is double taxation, since both the corporate entity and the individual owners have to file tax returns. As you will see, this may be avoided with a Subchapter S Corporation.

- Record-keeping requirements can be more extensive with a corporation.

- Operating across state lines can be complicated because corporations need to "qualify to do business" in states where they are not incorporated. This is explained later in greater detail.

- Ending the corporate existence, and in many cases even changing the structure of the organization, can be more complicated and costly than for partnerships and proprietorships.

The selection of the form of organization of a business should be decided with professional assistance. Nevertheless, the prevailing attitude is that a corporation is the preferred form of organization, since its advantages far outweigh its disadvantages.

> *note*
> Unlike a sole proprietorship or partnership, the corporation continues to exist even if an owner (shareholder) dies or sells his shares of the business.

This guide takes you through the incorporation process. Once you have decided that the corporation is the correct form of organization for your business, you must go through the legal steps required to create your corporation. These steps vary from state to state. They also vary in complexity. But with careful planning, most people can organize their own corporation without a lawyer, thus saving hundreds of dollars in legal fees.

Where to incorporate

Chapter 2

Where to incorporate

What you'll find in this chapter:

➤ The Delaware advantage

➤ Nevada and Wyoming's appeal

➤ The foreign corporation

➤ Other factors to consider

➤ The registered agent

The first question is to decide the state within which to organize the corporation. Most businesses incorporate in the state where they are located, however, there are some advantages to incorporating outside of your state. You can choose from all 50 states and the District of Columbia.

You may have heard of the great advantages of incorporating in the state of Delaware, and it is true that a great percentage of the publicly held corporations in this country are incorporated there. There are reasons for this, many of which are no longer valid for public corporations, and most of which never had importance for a small corporation. As a matter of fact, many large Delaware corporations started out in other states. Only when they grew in size to become large national corporations did they move their "corporate entity" to Delaware.

Delaware's Division of Incorporations suggests these advantages to incorporating in that state:

- the franchise tax compares favorably with that of any other state

- shares of stock owned by persons outside of the state are not subject to taxation

- shares of stock that are part of the estate of a non-resident decedent are exempt from the state Inheritance Tax Law

- Delaware courts construe the Corporation Law liberally, allowing investors confidence in the security of their investment

- directors have greater statutory protection from liability in Delaware

> **note** If your business is in another state, there would have to be overwhelming advantages to incorporating in Delaware, because the business is now subject to the regulations of two states.

Although the above advantages are true, it does not necessarily follow that Delaware should be the location of your corporation. There are many reasons for incorporating elsewhere. First, of course, is that most corporations will operate businesses located somewhere else in the country and are not likely ever to do business in Delaware.

note If your business is, for example, going to be a retail store in New York City, it would be more advisable to set up a New York corporation. If you were to set up a Delaware corporation and operate a store in New York City, you would still have to qualify "to do business" in the state of New York, which would then require:

- filing an application to do business as a "foreign," or out-of-state, corporation

- paying franchise taxes as a foreign corporation in New York

- reporting and paying annual taxes in New York as well as Delaware

If you plan to do business outside your company's resident state, you may have to qualify as a foreign corporation in every state where you do business. Later we will discuss what constitutes "doing business" and when your business requires such qualification in various states. Needless to say, incorporating in the state where you are located makes the greatest sense.

Favorable Delaware Corporation Law was more a reason for incorporating there in the past than it is now. It is true that at one time Delaware had the most liberal statute in the country for corporations, which allowed the management of a corporation great flexibility in the operations of the business. Nevertheless, this flexibility is most valuable for corporations that have thousands of stockholders all over the world. It is fairly meaningless to the small corporation that is not publicly owned.

Furthermore, other states have revised their own Corporation Laws so that the advantages that once were available only in Delaware are available in many states. Nevada and Wyoming are such states, and have become even more popular than Delaware as states within which to incorporate. Nevada offers lower taxes, no corporate franchise fees and more protection and privacy for corporate officers, directors and stockholders than does Delaware.

User-friendly Nevada and Wyoming

Which states are friendliest to corporations? Most people say Delaware, but they are mistaken. Nevada offers many advantages over Delaware and all other states, except Wyoming, whose corporation laws closely parallel Nevada's. There are many advantages in choosing to incorporate in Nevada rather than Delaware:

• Delaware taxes corporate profits. Nevada is tax-free. Delaware will be more costly if you expect significant profits.

• Nevada will not share tax information with the IRS. Other states, including Delaware, do exchange information.

• Delaware has a franchise tax, but Nevada does not.

• Delaware requires extensive annual disclosure, including stockholder meeting dates, business localities outside Delaware and the number and value of shares issued. Nevada requires no such information, only the current list of officers and directors.

• Nevada's corporate officers and directors have far broader protection than do Delaware's. Articles of incorporation in Nevada may eliminate or limit the personal liability of officers and directors for breach of fiduciary duty, other than improper dividend payments. Nevada also has a shorter statute of limitations to sue for improper dividends and more options for director indemnification. Delaware director indemnification is at the court's discretion. It is an absolute right in Nevada.

Stockholders are not public record in Nevada, and shares may be held in bearer form with ownership anonymous.

• Nevada also allows broader indemnities to others who incur liability on behalf of the corporation. Insurance trust funds, self-insurance and granting directors a security interest or lien on corporate assets to guarantee their indemnifications are common examples. For asset protection, the absolute authority of corporate officers and directors to place liens on their own corporate assets for indemnification purposes provides them continuing control over their corporate assets without the need to prove an exchange of funds. *This is an important strategy!* Delaware and all other states invalidate such self-serving financial and legal arrangements. Absent fraud, a Nevada board of directors' decision concerning financial arrangements is conclusive and is neither void nor voidable. This is untrue in Delaware and elsewhere.

• It is also quite easy to incorporate in Nevada. Because so many astute business owners now establish Nevada corporations, many firms offer complete incorporation and resident agent services to clients nationwide.

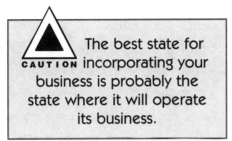 The best state for incorporating your business is probably the state where it will operate its business.

If you incorporate in another state, including Delaware or Nevada, you must also register to conduct business as a foreign corporation in your own state. Your corporation then becomes subject to the laws of your state which voids the advantages of incorporating in Nevada or Wyoming. Your business may additionally incur multiple state taxes and filing requirements.

 Consider Nevada or Wyoming only when your corporation will not regularly do business elsewhere or remains a passive operating entity.

The one downside of the Nevada corporation is that they are most frequently IRS audited. Wyoming offers the same corporate advantages as Nevada, and reportedly has fewer IRS audits.

Other considerations

Base your decision regarding where to incorporate on the important factors. The location of your physical facilities can be the most important factor. Consider the costs of incorporating in that state, and if you incorporate in a state other than the one you're physically located in, consider what it will cost to become authorized to do business in that state.

These costs include fees to check and reserve the name you want to use for your corporation, the cost of filing incorporation papers, and whether there is a one-time organizational fee or franchise tax (this is often based upon the number of shares you will have authorized for the corporation to issue).

In addition to the initial costs, you must determine what the annual fees are in the states you are considering. For example, if there is an annual report to file with the secretary of state, what is the filing fee? Is there an annual franchise tax? Is there a state or local income tax, and how is it determined?

The laws governing corporations in your state of choice also can be another important factor. For example, some states require three incorporators and three directors. If you plan to have a corporation owned or controlled by one person, your state may require you to have more board members than you want. These requirements vary from state to state; in almost all instances, however, it is advisable for a small business corporation to organize within the state where business will actually be conducted, as it is usually easy to comply with those corporate requirements. Consideration of other states is only recommended when the business will, in fact, do business in other states.

E-Z TIP A publication titled Martindale-Hubbell Law Directory, found in public and law libraries, contains summaries of the laws of all 50 states. You should read the incorporation statutes for the appropriate state before filing your incorporation papers.

Once you have decided what state to incorporate in, a great deal of information about how to set up that corporation free or for minimal fees can be obtained from the appropriate secretary of state. A listing of the address and telephone number of the department to contact in your state is contained in the Resources section of this guide.

The registered agent

States generally require that their corporations maintain a registered agent in the state in order to receive communications and summonses in the event of a lawsuit. Generally, this agent may be the office of the corporation itself. If you are physically located in the state of incorporation, the corporation itself or an officer would be the registered agent.

If you incorporate in a state where you do not actually have an office, you need a local agent. There are many organizations in the business of representing corporations for a small annual fee. These are easily found in law directories.

Selection and reservation of the corporate name

3

Chapter 3

Selection and reservation of the corporate name

What you'll find in this chapter:

➠ Words you cannot use in your name

➠ Words you must have in your name

➠ Choosing a descriptive name

➠ "Deceptively similar"

➠ Reserving your corporate name

Once you are ready to set up your own corporation, you must next select a corporate name and then check to see if the state in which you are going to incorporate will allow you to use the name.

The first obstacle, other than your own originality, will be the state statutes that prohibit the use of certain words. Not all states have the same prohibitions, so you should check your particular state. However, words that typically cannot be used include:

acceptance	endowment	national
architect	engineering	pharmacy
bank	federal	savings
banking	guaranty	state police

board of trade	indemnity	thrift
certified accountant	insurance	trust
chamber of commerce	lawyer	underwriter
cooperative	loan	United States
credit union	medical	urban development
doctor	mortgage	urban relocation

These words are, of course, used in the names of organizations or corporations, but only in fields in which special licensing or regulation is required. Such corporations must be organized pursuant to statutes regulating their particular fields. It is not advisable to attempt to set up such a corporation without the assistance of a lawyer.

note When choosing your corporate name, you should also check what must be included.

All states require that a corporate name include an indication of limited liability so that people dealing with the organization know that if it fails, they cannot collect their debts from the owners personally. The words that indicate this are:

Association	Club	Institute
Company	Foundation	Limited
Co.	Fund	Ltd.
Corporation	Incorporated	Society
Corp.	Inc.	Syndicate

This requirement should be checked carefully before selecting the name. New York, for example, allows only Corporation, Incorporated, Limited or their abbreviations.

Once you've decided on a name, you must investigate whether the name you want is already being used by someone else. Even similar names can cause problems, because most states will not allow a name that is the

 note Always clear the proposed corporate name before you prepare and file your corporate papers.

same or "deceptively similar" to a name already on record in the state. Therefore, your XYZ Corp. restaurant may be a problem, for example, if there is already an XYZ Inc. bakery in the state.

One useful thing to keep in mind is to choose a descriptive word and a proper name for your corporation. Perhaps XYZ Restaurant Corp., or XYZ Foods Corp., in the above example, would be accepted, whereas XYZ Corp. might be refused on the basis of its being "deceptively similar" to the XYZ, Inc. already in existence.

The materials you obtain from the secretary of state will help you learn how to reserve the name. Usually it is done by submitting a letter or a form with the required fee and waiting to receive clearance. In some cases you can check the availability of the name with a telephone call.

Types of corporate stock

4

Chapter 4

Types of corporate stock

> **What you'll find in this chapter:**
>
> ⟱➤ The corporate stockholder
> ⟱➤ Common stock
> ⟱➤ Preferred stock
> ⟱➤ No-par value stock
> ⟱➤ Par value stock

The stockholders of a corporation are the owners of the corporation. When a business incorporates, it issues units of stock indicating who owns what "share" of the incorporated business. These shares are paid for, in turn, with money, property, or services. Thus, if a corporation's net worth is $30,000, and there are 300 shares issued, each share would be worth $100. If there are two people who each own 150 shares of the stock, then each person (shareholder) owns half of the corporation.

The main types of stock a corporation may issue are:

- common stock
- preferred stock
- no-par value stock
- par value stock

> **E-Z TIP**
>
> It is wise to reserve about half the authorized shares, as you will not have to amend the corporate charter when admitting additional investors to the corporation.

Common stock

DEFINITION

Holders of *common stock* are entitled to have the primary voice in selecting directors. Voting rights are attached to each share of stock, usually one vote per share. Furthermore, common stockholders are entitled to share in the profits and in final distribution of the corporate assets on dissolution.

> *note*
>
> More than one kind, or "class," of common stock may be issued. Certain conditions may be imposed upon each class, such as restrictions on voting rights. Common stock is designated in terms of what rights its owners may be entitled to.

Preferred stock

DEFINITION

The holders of *preferred stock* are usually entitled to "preference" over the holders of common stock with respect to receipt of dividends and distribution of assets upon the dissolution of the corporation. They usually do not have voting rights, however. Preferred shares are generally not issued by smaller corporations. Cumulative preferred stock entitles the preferred stockholder to receive all accumulated back dividends before any dividends are received by the common stockholders.

For our purposes in this guide, and for the purposes of most small or medium-sized corporations, only common stock is important and one class of common stock is generally sufficient. For a small or medium-sized corporation it is not necessary to authorize or issue a large number of shares of common stock; the minimum number of shares allowed under the state law will be sufficient for most purposes. Beyond this minimum, the state usually imposes a proportionately higher filing fee and tax.

No-par value stock

DEFINITION

No-par value stock bears no stated or nominal value on the face of the stock certificate; hence, it does not purport to represent anything more than the given number of shares or ownership interest in the corporation. The actual value represented by the stock will depend, therefore, on what an investor is willing to pay for it, based on such factors as the product line or the assets of the corporation, the profitability of its business, the quality of its management, its record of past performance and dividend payouts, etc.

Par value stock

DEFINITION

Par value stock, on the other hand, bears a stated or nominal value on the face of the stock certificate (i.e., $10), which represents the amount contributed by the shareholder(s) to buy each share of stock. Because the value of any share of stock generally fluctuates from day to day, the "par value" of stock can be misleading if used to measure the worth of a stock. Merely because a share of stock says it has a "$10 par value" does not necessarily mean the stock is actually worth that amount.

Drafting a corporate purpose

Chapter 5

Drafting a corporate purpose

What you'll find in this chapter:

⏩ The corporate purpose

⏩ Deciding on your corporation's objectives

⏩ Avoiding extra filings

⏩ Allowing for future contingencies

⏩ Examples of a corporate purpose

In order to incorporate, it is necessary to record the purpose of your company. Great care should be taken when stating the intended purpose of the proposed corporation, since the activities of the corporation may be unduly limited unless carefully written to be as broad and inclusive as possible. When the powers granted to the corporation are not broad enough for its needs, the corporation must petition the state to amend its corporate charter (Articles) by filing a Certificate of Amendment before it may expand its activities beyond those originally approved.

To draft appropriate purposes and activities for the corporation, follow these two steps:

1) Write down a statement setting forth the specific objectives, purposes, and activities the corporation will engage in, including all related lines of business.

2) Add the statement below to allow for future contingencies and to protect the right of the corporation to expand future activities:

The foregoing purposes and activities will be interpreted as examples only and not as limitations, and nothing therein shall be deemed as prohibiting the corporation from extending its activities to any related or otherwise permissible lawful business purposes which may become necessary, profitable or desirable for the furtherance of the corporate objectives expressed above.

The following examples illustrate how two different businesses might state their corporate purposes.

1) Construction business

Purposes: To engage in the construction, repair and remodeling of buildings and public works of all kinds, and in the improvement of real estate, and in doing any other business and contracting work incidental to or connected with such work, including demolition.

note Not-for-profit (or non-profit) or educational corporations usually have to submit additional documents to clarify their intended corporate purpose.

The foregoing purposes and activities will be interpreted as examples only and not as limitations, and nothing therein shall be deemed as prohibiting the corporation from extending its activities to any related or otherwise permissible lawful business purposes which may become necessary, profitable or desirable for the furtherance of the corporate objectives expressed above.

2) General merchandising business

Purposes: To manufacture, produce, purchase or otherwise acquire, sell, import, export, distribute and deal in goods, wares, merchandise and materials of any kind and description.

The foregoing purposes and activities will be interpreted as examples only and not as limitations, and nothing therein shall be deemed as prohibiting the corporation from extending its activities to any related or otherwise permissible lawful business purposes which may become necessary, profitable or desirable for the furtherance of the corporate objectives expressed above.

Choosing a fiscal year

Chapter 6

Choosing a fiscal year

What you'll find in this chapter:

➠ The Employer Identification Number (EIN)

➠ Choosing the right fiscal year for you

➠ The calendar year, and other choices

➠ Taxes and your fiscal year

➠ Making the most of tax savings

DEFINITION IRS form SS-4, Application for Employer Identification Number, asks you to state your *fiscal year*, the 12 months of your financial activity upon which the IRS bases its tax calculations. In some states, you are also required to state your fiscal year on your Certificate of Incorporation. Form SS-4 is available at your local IRS office, by phone or online; see the Resources section of this guide.

It is easiest to choose the calendar year as your corporation's fiscal year, since you will have fewer tax forms to file that way. However, there are several tax advantages to choosing a fiscal year that is not the calendar year.

E-Z TIP When corresponding with the IRS, be sure to include your Employer Identification Number (EIN). The EIN identifies your business to the IRS.

You might want to choose July 1 to June 30. In that case, for your first year of incorporation you would have to file two sets of income tax forms: For the first half of the year you would file as a sole proprietor (individual return) using Schedule C and any other appropriate schedules; for the second half of the year you would file a corporate return (Form 1120, or Form 1120S, if you make the Subchapter S election), and an individual return because you are now an employee of your corporation.

There are still other choices for your fiscal year:

- If you choose April 1 or October 1 as the beginning of your fiscal year, you will have to file the same two sets of tax returns for your first year of incorporation.

- If you choose April 1, you would file as a sole proprietor for the first quarter (January 1 to March 31), and you would file corporate and individual returns for the last three quarters (April 1 to December 31).

- If you choose October 1 you would file as a sole proprietor for the first three quarters (January 1 to September 30), and you would file corporate and individual returns for the last quarter (October 1 to December 31).

Fiscal year and taxes

The advantage of separate years is that it allows flexibility in tax planning. For instance, you can contract the amount of salary you pay yourself as late as December 31 and have it taxed personally. If you decide on a small amount, it will reduce your personal tax accordingly, leave money

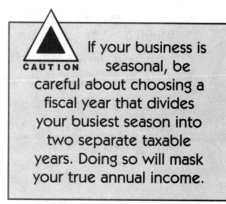

CAUTION If your business is seasonal, be careful about choosing a fiscal year that divides your busiest season into two separate taxable years. Doing so will mask your true annual income.

in the corporation for its use, and gain additional time to find a suitable tax angle to avoid paying the resultant corporate tax—a business trip, for example, which is deductible and reduces corporate profits.

 And the tax savings of separate years, both corporate and personal, can be significant. You may want to choose a fiscal year by following the advice of your accountant, who can determine the fiscal year most advantageous to you.

The corporate board and directors

7

Chapter 7

The corporate board and directors

What you'll find in this chapter:

- The corporate board of directors
- How the board of directors functions
- Directors and stockholders
- Liability of directors
- The corporate officers

The management of a corporation consists of the corporate directors and the corporate officers.

Corporate directors

Subject to any restrictions imposed by the corporate charter or bylaws, the right and responsibility to determine policy and conduct the business of the corporation lies with the board of directors. The number of those who make up the board is usually set by the bylaws of the corporation.

Bylaws are drawn up and adopted at the first meeting of the stockholders. The directors are elected by the stockholders and are ultimately responsible to the stockholders. Stockholders have the power to remove directors, with or without cause, when the charter of incorporation or the bylaws so authorize and at any special meeting of the stockholders called for that purpose. Directors are usually elected at the annual meeting of stockholders.

> **note** Some states limit the length of time a director may serve. States do not, however, prevent a director from running for re-election.

It is important to remember that stockholders actually vote their shares of stock. Thus, if there are three stockholders but one owns 80 percent of the shares of stock, that stockholder (the majority stockholder) will control the vote based on the amount of stock ownership.

If any restrictions imposed on the general powers of the directors are contained in the corporation's charter, third persons, such as creditors, are also bound by them, since the charter is considered a public record. Restrictions embodied only in the corporate bylaws, however, are not binding upon third persons, as bylaws are not publicly filed or recorded.

Directors must act as a body. They can bind the corporation only by actions taken at a board meeting with the necessary quorum. They cannot vote by proxy and their duties generally may not be delegated to others. A resolution not passed at a board meeting but signed by each individual director at his or her home would be invalid, unless the directors were the sole stockholders.

> **note** If all the corporate shares are owned by fewer than three people, the number of directors generally must not be fewer than the number of stockholders in the corporation.

The directors are generally required by law to meet at least once every year, although as a practical matter this is rarely done in family or small corporations. In such meetings of the directors, the directors appoint the corporate officers (the same officers are often re-elected), ratify acts of the prior year, review important business matters and set broad policy objectives. The corporate secretary then writes up minutes as a record of the meetings.

The directors may also authorize dividends, a new contract, a new lease, a loan, or major purchases or projects. Such actions are then recorded as corporate resolutions and are formally recorded in the minutes book of the corporation.

> *note* The law does not require that corporate minutes follow a particular format. Nevertheless, whatever format is chosen, it should be used consistently.

As a practical matter, minutes of directors' and stockholders' meetings are often very helpful as an instrument of management, since they are frequently the only official record of what was done or decided upon by these bodies. When accurately and adequately kept, the minutes may help avoid misunderstandings or potential lawsuits.

Provided the board of directors acts honestly, the directors can generally bind the corporation by actions taken at board meetings and are not personally liable for any such actions. Hence, if an honest but bad or imprudent judgment should result in business losses, the directors may not be held personally liable unless the action was grossly negligent or made in bad faith.

Directors may be personally liable if they:

- exploit their office for personal gain at the expense of the corporation or of its stockholders. The directors are usually said to have a "fiduciary" relationship with the stockholders, meaning one that presumes the utmost good faith and trust.

> *note* Directors would generally not be liable if they reasonably relied upon corporate records fraudulently prepared by an employee.

- wrongfully dispose of corporate assets or declare and pay dividends when no surplus or profit exists

- authorize the issue of unissued stock to themselves for the purpose of converting themselves from minority to majority stockholders

- issue, as fully paid, shares of stock not paid for

- improperly lend corporate funds to stockholders when such funds remain unpaid or uncollectible

Corporate officers

The president, vice president, treasurer and secretary (and such other officers as the particular corporation may choose to have) are appointed by the board of directors; their salaries, duties and conditions of employment are fixed by the board.

The officers run and manage the corporation from day to day. However, they have only such legitimate responsibilities and authority to act on behalf of the board of directors as are conferred upon them by the board, or as are specified in the bylaws of the corporation.

Corporations are required to have a president, treasurer and secretary (or clerk). Other officers, such as chairperson, vice president, or assistant treasurer, are optional and are not usually included in the Articles of Incorporation.

President

Also known as the chief executive officer (CEO), the President is responsible for the day-to-day operations of the corporation.

Vice-President

The Vice-President has no specific authority until given such by the board or the corporation's bylaws. A vice-president generally fills in for the president when he/she is unavailable.

Treasurer

The treasurer has custody of corporate funds with the responsibility to receive and disburse those funds. This officer may not, however, borrow money or issue negotiable instrument on his own.

Secretary

The secretary is responsible for record keeping and reporting of meetings, including voting records and minutes. Corporate secretaries also conduct corporate elections and tabulate votes.

The Certificate or Articles of Incorporation

8

Chapter 8

The Certificate or Articles of Incorporation

What you'll find in this chapter:

➡ Items in the Certificate of Incorporation

➡ State requirements

➡ Professional and non-profit corporations

➡ What to do once you have filed

➡ The corporate seal and stock certificates

You are now ready to prepare and file a Certificate of Incorporation (in many states it is titled Articles of Incorporation). Many states will supply you with a blank form or with a model form that must be retyped. Note: Call the secretary of state in the state where you intend to incorporate to determine whether a specific state form is required.

E-Z Tip

If no specific form is required by your state, find out what information is required in the Certificate or Articles of Incorporation and draft your own.

The following items of information are typically required in a Certificate of Incorporation:

- name and address of the corporation

- fiscal year

- purposes of the corporation

- total number of shares authorized for issuance (including the par value of shares, and the classes of shares if more than one class)

- preferences, limitations, and relative rights of each class of stock

- initial capital paid into the corporation

- number of directors constituting initial board of directors

- name and address of each of the initial directors

- name and address of the president, treasurer and secretary

- name and address of each incorporator

note

Not all of these items may be required in your state, and many will not apply or be appropriate in your case. Some states, e.g., South Carolina, require that an attorney certify that your Articles of Incorporation conform to your state's statutory requirements. The only way to be certain of the requirements is to call your secretary of state and ask for a sample Certificate of Incorporation. See the Resources section of this guide for the appropriate telephone number in your state.

Special corporations

For the purposes of this guide we have limited our discussion to business corporations. Professional corporations and corporations in highly regulated industries may require more complicated corporate documents. People in those fields should seek legal counsel in setting up their businesses.

note All signatures on the Certificate of Incorporation must be originals. Photocopies are not accepted.

We have also not covered not-for-profit corporations, since the procedures are even more complicated. In many states approvals must be sought from numerous state agencies to begin a charitable corporation, and the procedure for obtaining a tax exemption may require the aid of professionals familiar with that area of tax law. There are many groups of volunteer lawyers around the country that will organize charitable corporations for free. Check with your local bar association or local or state arts council for the names of such volunteers.

Once your Certificate of Incorporation has been drafted and signed, it should be mailed or delivered to the secretary of state's office or other state office as is proper, along with the required fees. The fee is usually based on the number of pages in the certificate and usually costs only a few dollars.

> **note** Your Certificate of Incorporation may be amended at any time by filing the required forms with the proper fees.

You will be notified by return mail that the certificate has been accepted and filed. Your evidence of filing is generally a receipt from the state. You may also request a copy of the Certificate of Incorporation with the state certificate of filing and the official incorporation date.

Your first order of business

Once the documents have been filed, the incorporator should hold the initial meeting of the corporation, elect the board of directors and turn the management of the corporation over to it. In many states the initial board of directors must be listed in the Certificate of Incorporation. The incorporators' meeting, depending on state law, may be an actual meeting or may be evidenced by a signed statement of action.

Certain states allow the board (and the stockholders) to transact business without actually meeting if they all sign a written statement setting forth the action they have transacted. Some states allow a meeting to take place with the directors communicating by a conference telephone call. In this way they can be all over the world and still legally conduct business. Check the law in your state to see if these types of meetings or consents are legal.

The initial activity of the board of directors will include such start-up activities as:

- electing the officers

- opening a bank account

- adopting a corporate seal and form of a stock certificate

- issuing stock

The corporate seal is a simple impression seal that usually contains the name of the corporation, the year of incorporation and the state of incorporation. It can be bought at most stationery or office supply stores at a nominal cost.

note
Most states no longer require a corporate seal, nor do they require that the seal be applied to corporate documents. The decision to adopt a seal is up to the corporation.

Additional stock certificates from Made E-Z Products™ are also available at office supply stores nationwide. Check your state's laws to make certain you include all the required information on your stock certificate. Usually it must include the name of the corporation, the state of incorporation, the type of stock (common, preferred, etc.), the par value of the shares, any preferences that these or other shares have, the name of the holder, the signatures of officers of the corporation, and the corporate seal.

Establishing your corporation

Chapter 9

Establishing your corporation

What you'll find in this chapter:

➡ The incorporation checklist

➡ Notifying customers and creditors

➡ Complying with requirements

➡ Records and bank accounts

➡ Determining if you are "doing business"

Steps in the incorporation process:

1) decide whether to incorporate

2) decide where to incorporate

3) select a corporate name

4) select a registered agent, if necessary

5) draft a Certificate or Articles of Incorporation

6) sign the Certificate of Incorporation, and file with the secretary of state along with the appropriate filing fees

7) hold incorporator's initial meeting to elect directors and transact first business

8) hold organizational meeting of initial board of directors

9) select a corporate seal and stock certificates, issue shares, elect officers, and open bank accounts

10) apply for an Employer Identification Number

11) choose a fiscal year

12) file a "doing business as" certificate, if necessary

13) apply for authorization to do business in other states, if necessary

14) obtain necessary state and local licenses and/or permits

15) determine eligibility as an S corporation

16) hold regular, official meetings of directors and stockholders

17) document actions and maintain accurate corporate records

With your corporation organized, how do you operate and manage it? Listed below are a few guiding pointers.

Transfer assets to the corporation

If you have been operating a business prior to incorporation (as many people do) you can transfer the assets and debts of the business to the new corporation for an agreed sum or consideration, and receive shares of stock in exchange. All gifts to the corporation should be acknowledged by corporate resolution or by letter describing the gift, its value and the date of the gift. You cannot, however, burden the corporation with more debts than assets. Further, you cannot sell your

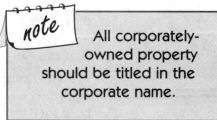

note — All corporately-owned property should be titled in the corporate name.

personal property to the corporation at inflated prices, or exchange its stock for personal property that is overvalued.

Notify your customers

A sound business practice is to notify all existing business associates, creditors and customers or clients of the change to a corporate status. This can be done by personal communication (telephone or letter) or by a small newspaper notice. Generally, all subsequent company records and transactions should be changed to reflect the new corporate status of the organization, including the printing of new letterheads, business cards, stationery, signs, advertising, telephone numbers and web sites..

Determine state and local requirements

The parties starting a new business must consider not only the formalities of incorporation, but other possible regulations and requirements. Permits and licenses, for example, are required for such businesses as real estate brokers, barbers, hairdressers, private investigators, cosmetologists, billiard rooms, pharmacies, nursing homes, notaries, peddlers, newsstands, employment agencies, businesses serving or selling alcoholic beverages, health concerns, hospitals and educational institutions.

Many businesses are regulated by federal agencies, such as brokerage and securities businesses, air transportation, banking, and drug manufacturing companies. Before commencing any new business, consider what regulations are applicable so that your business will not be conducted in violation of these rules and regulations.

In addition, any business that hires employees must consider personnel issues such as:

- whether it is subject to rules relating to withholding of taxes for local, state and federal governments

- whether it must pay Social Security tax, unemployment insurance or workers' compensation

- whether any unions have jurisdiction and what pension or other payments must be made to them

- whether minimum wage requirements are applicable

- whether hiring minors is permissible

- any occupational safety and health regulations

Be open to advice

There are a number of federal and local agencies besides the office of the secretary of state that can assist you in incorporating your business.

First is your state department of securities and the regional office of the Securities and Exchange Commission. These agencies regulate the sale of securities. In most start-ups of small businesses, the number of owners of stock is so few that neither the state nor federal governments need be involved. They usually become involved only when you are selling stock to more than 25 people or making what is known as a "public offering." However, even with fewer stockholders, there may be questions as to whether your stock sale or your proposed financing must be cleared with the authorities.

The Small Business Administration of the federal government was established by Congress in 1953 to provide prospective, new, and established members of the small business community with financial and management training and counseling. Check your Yellow Pages for their local office. Counseling sponsored by the Service Corps Of Retired Executives (SCORE) is extremely helpful, and they may offer free on-site counseling services, workshops and seminars. Also contact your local trade associations and the local chamber of commerce. They, too, can give you much advice and assistance.

Keep separate corporate records

Remember that your corporation is viewed in the eyes of the law as a different "legal entity," separate and apart from the owner(s). Hence, to avoid potential IRS problems, you must maintain separate sets of records, one for your personal affairs and one for the affairs of the corporation. As a rule, however, it is not necessary to maintain an elaborate bookkeeping system. A separate bank account and bookkeeping that clearly show what you and the corporation separately earn and pay out is usually sufficient. A local bookkeeper or accountant can set up a convenient accounting and tax system for your business.

Set up your corporate bank accounts

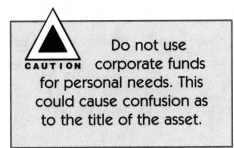
CAUTION Do not use corporate funds for personal needs. This could cause confusion as to the title of the asset.

To open a corporate bank account, you need an Employer Identification Number for your corporation. To obtain this, file application form SS-4 with the IRS. If you already have an EIN (Employer

Identification Number) for a Keogh Plan account or because you have had employees in an unincorporated business, you nevertheless need a new number for the corporation, as the corporation is a new person or entity. The bank will probably also require a Corporate Resolution, duly signed with the corporate seal, as an official corporate indication of authorization to open a bank account.

Verify whether you're doing business in another state

If your new corporation is strictly a local business, it is unlikely that you will need to be authorized or qualified to do business in another state. You clearly are doing business in only one place.

But what happens if you start advertising in magazines and you get orders from out of state? Are you now doing business in more than one state? Or what if you are in the sales business, have a store or sales office in only one place, but have sales representatives who drive to other states and call on potential customers? Does this mean you are now doing business elsewhere? If you start expanding and open up new stores, then you would clearly be doing business in these other locations.

Before we go further into how you decide whether you are doing business in another state, let's look at why it matters. If you are doing business in another state but have not qualified by filing the proper papers and paying the fees, the consequences can be serious. In all states, an unqualified foreign corporation is denied access to the courts of the state, which would mean you could not sue someone in that state to enforce a contract or obligation. In addition, many states impose fines when they discover a corporation doing business without being qualified; in some cases, directors, officers or agents may be subject to these fines. These consequences could be serious for your business.

The statutes of many states define what constitutes "doing business" within that state. While engaging in interstate commerce by itself does not constitute "doing business" within a state, if you engage in such interstate commerce and have a registered office, address or agent in a state other than the one in which you are incorporated, you need to register in that state as a foreign corporation. Other principal business activities considered "doing business" are:

- soliciting and receiving orders by mail within that state

- soliciting orders within that state through an agent, sales representative or independent contractor

- shipping orders from a warehouse within that state

- paying state taxes

- accepting service of process

> *note* If you do have to become authorized to do business as a foreign corporation, the procedure is relatively simple. Obtain the application form from the secretary of state, complete it, and file it with the proper fees.

Since requirements vary from state to state, you should consult the statutes in any state in which you contemplate one or more of the above activities.

The Model Corporation Act

The Model Corporation Act, drafted by a group of lawyers and law professors, gives a list of activities that, in and of themselves, do not constitute "doing business." Since this act is the basis for the laws in many states, it is a good guide as to what activities you can do *without* having to qualify as a business in another state. The language reads as follows:

Without excluding other activities which may not constitute transacting business in this state, a foreign corporation shall not be considered to be transacting business in this state, for the purposes of this Act, by reason of carrying on in this state any one or more of the following activities:

- *Maintaining or defending any action or suit or any administrative or arbitration proceeding, or effecting the settlement thereof or the settlement of claims or disputes.*

- *Holding meetings of its directors or shareholders or carrying on other activities concerning its internal affairs.*

- *Maintaining bank accounts.*

- *Maintaining offices or agencies for the transfer, exchange and registration of its securities or appointing and maintaining trustees or depositories with relation to its securities.*

- *Effecting sales through independent contractors.*

- *Soliciting or procuring orders, whether by mail or through employees or agents or otherwise, where such orders require acceptance without this state before becoming binding contracts.*

- *Creating as borrower or lender, or acquiring indebtedness or mortgages or other security interests in real or personal property.*

- *Securing or collecting debts or enforcing any rights in property securing the same.*

- *Transacting any business in interstate commerce.*

- *Conducting an isolated transaction completed within a period of thirty days and not in the course of a number of repeated transactions of like nature.*

The "S Corporation" election

10

Chapter 10

The "S Corporation" election

DEFINITION

An *S Corporation* (previously a Subchapter S Corporation, also called a Small Business Corporation) is, for most tax purposes, treated by the IRS as if it were a partnership or sole proprietorship. This means that it is not a tax-paying entity, as a regular C Corporation is.

If you form a C Corporation, the profits of that business are taxed twice. First the corporation pays a corporate tax on the profit. Then, when the after-tax profit is distributed to you as a shareholder, you pay a hefty income tax on it as dividend income. This is the double taxation that is imposed on corporate profits.

The S Corporation, on the other hand, is viewed only as a financial channel through which its income, deductions, credits and losses are passed to its shareholders. It is these shareholders who must pay whatever tax is due. If at the end of the year your S Corporation earns a profit, it does not pay any taxes on that profit. Instead, the profit is considered *your* income and *you* pay the tax.

Can you benefit from an S Corporation?

Virtually every type of business operation can benefit by being operated as an S Corporation, with the possible exception of businesses that expect to retain rather than distribute profits. Because it is treated as a partnership, an S Corporation must report that its shareholders have earned profits even if it does not distribute these profits. But even in this situation, the fact that individual tax rates are lower than corporate rates may justify a decision in favor of the S Corporation.

note Because it is taxed as a partnership, it is frequently believed that the S corporation loses the limited liability feature of a corporation. This is untrue. Consider only the tax consequences when choosing your type of corporation.

How and when to use an S Corporation

Use of the S Corporation should depend upon several factors:

- the type of business that you own

- the profitability of your business

- your personal tax bracket

- the types of assets used by your business

- the growth prospects for your business

- the recognition of an S Corporation by your state

Which businesses benefit most?

◆ service industries with modest equipment or capital asset requirements

◆ fully developed businesses that will not require additional capital investments

◆ enterprises that will invest in real estate, equipment, or other property that will rapidly appreciate in value

◆ start-up ventures that are expected to operate at a loss for the first year or two

When to be taxed as a regular corporation

Forming an S Corporation is one of many tax strategies available to small-business owners. Like other tax-saving techniques, it is not recommended in all cases. You should decide to be taxed as a regular corporation when:

- Your business becomes profitable and you want to build up your company earnings to expand your business.

- You have owned a profitable service business for several years and, rather than drain the earnings from the company, you now want to accumulate them in the corporation and diversify. Regular corporate tax rates may leave more cash for reinvestment. Of course, it may be possible to pull sufficient income out of the corporation as salary to avoid double taxation.

- You formed your S Corporation several years ago as a tax shelter. The shelter's earnings have risen and it is now about to become very profitable, throwing these profits into your high-bracket personal return. The solution is to give up S Corporation status and let the profits be taxed at corporate rates.

- There are considerable passive losses, such as through tax credits, depreciation, or real estate investments. Even though these losses result from accounting strategies, the items should be taken out of the S Corporation and placed under the ownership of a C Corporation or held personally.

- There are more than 75 shareholders in your S Corporation. (stock in the S Corporation that is jointly held by a husband and wife is treated as if owned by one shareholder). Since 75 is the maximum limit allowed by law, beyond this number your S Corporation will automatically revert back to C Corporation status.

S corporation warning signs

Some of the potential drawbacks to forming an S Corporation include:

- You risk losing your S Corporation status if one of your stockholders transfers shares to a trust, partnership or corporation.

- If any new stockholder files a formal refusal to consent to the S corporation election, the status S will be lost.

- You will lose your S Corporation status if stock is accidentally sold to more stockholders than permitted by law.

- Your S Corporation must, in any one year, receive 80 percent or less of its gross revenue from inside the U.S. or S Corporation status will be terminated.

- If in any one year, 20 percent or more of gross revenues come from passive income such as: royalties, rents, dividends, interest, annuities, or profits from the sale of securities, S Corporation status is terminated.

Should your corporation lose its S status, additional taxes and penalties will be levied against your company. These penalties will continue to accrue until the books are audited by the IRS.

The S Corporation and the LLC

The S Corporation is similar in many respects to the limited liability company. However, even though both types of business provide limited liability and similar tax advantages, there are eight important differences. Unlike a limited liability company, an S Corporation:

1) enjoys widespread popularity

2) may not own more than 80 percent of another corporation

3) may not have more than 75 shareholders

4) may not have more than one class of stock

5) may not have a non-resident alien, partnership, or corporation as a shareholder

6) can be acquired by another business, tax-free

7) owners pay employment taxes only on their salaries, not on all profits

8) state taxes may be lower

How to become an S corporation

1) Complete and file with the IRS a simple one-page form, IRS form 2553 (this permits tax filing as a small-business corporation).

2) Complete and file an individual tax return, IRS form 1120S, when it comes time to pay your taxes.

Form 2553 must be filed by the 15th day of the third month of the first taxable year. All S Corporations incorporated after 1982 must adopt the calendar year as their tax year, but they have some leeway as to a fiscal year within three months either side of a calendar year. These forms can be obtained at no charge by calling (or visiting) a local IRS Service Office.

Many small corporations are electing to be S Corporations because, under the new Tax Reform Act, individuals pay lower taxes than do corporations. Therefore, the business profits are more advantageously taxed at the lower individual rates. Nevertheless, the decision to become an S Corporation should be made after consulting with your attorney or accountant.

Maintaining corporate records

11

Chapter 11

Maintaining corporate records

> ### What you'll find in this chapter:
>
> ⇒ The importance of keeping good records
>
> ⇒ Minutes and amendments
>
> ⇒ Using resolution forms
>
> ⇒ Records of stockholder actions
>
> ⇒ Records of director actions

Once organized, the corporation must maintain a continuous record of all authorized actions approved by its stockholders or directors. Resolutions record the major decisions taken by the corporation's stockholders or board of directors.

While not always required, it is always a good idea to record your actions in the form of resolutions because they show outsiders that the actions were taken by and on behalf of the corporation. Keeping a careful

note Some resolutions are passed only by the stockholders; and others only by the Board of Directors. Some must be passed by both bodies.

record of corporate decisions is the single most important activity a corporation can take to ensure the legitimacy of the business it conducts.

Keep complete and detailed records

A complete and detailed record of stockholders' and directors' meetings, or minutes, as they are called, is important for many reasons:

- Parties dealing with the corporation may want evidence that the corporate action was approved.

- Officers and employees within the corporation are entitled to protection if their acts were approved.

- Accurate minutes are frequently necessary to preserve certain tax benefits or to avoid tax liabilities and penalties.

- Minutes are often necessary to prove that the corporation is operated as a separate entity independent of its principals.

Any changes to the corporation's Certificate or Articles of Incorporation must be approved by both the stockholders and directors. In addition to amendments, some states also require corporations to file a notarized affidavit which verifies the number of outstanding shares at the time of the vote. Stockholders must also vote to dissolve the corporation or to file for bankruptcy or reorganization.

note Amendments to the Certificate or Articles of Incorporation must be filed with the Secretary of State in the state of incorporation for the amendments to become effective.

Resolutions adopted by the board of directors that generally do not require stockholder approval involve everyday operations of the corporation, including but not limited to leasing, major purchases, hiring, banking, borrowing, investing, paying of dividends, salaries and bonuses, providing benefits for employees, and changing the corporate status, such as obtaining S corporation status.

 Made E-Z Products™ publishes *Corporate Record Keeping Made E-Z*, which contains forms to help you maintain a well-documented written record of stockholders' and directors' actions in a format that meets legal standards. By using either the book or software version, you can maintain an accurate minutes book and create a complete corporate biography, detailing the important events during the life of the corporation.

As a general rule, all records, resolutions and minutes of your corporation should be kept in your corporate minute book for a period of no less than six years. This is a good idea because sometimes a stockholder—and all stockholders have the right to do so—will want to inspect the corporate books and records to ensure the corporation is being run in its best interests. Your corporation should retain these records for a longer period should anyone ever challenge the actions of the board.

Resolution forms

Generally, you need only complete the resolution form that conforms to the corporate action voted upon. Occasionally, however, you may need to modify the form to suit your particular needs. Always be certain the resolution accurately states the corporate action approved. In some cases, particularly on more important transactions, you may find it necessary to have an attorney decide what the resolution should contain.

note While prepared forms can greatly simplify your record keeping requirements, they are not a substitute for your good judgment in deciding how you should document the actions of your corporation.

Records of stockholder actions

Stockholders can usually vote in person or by proxy, on the broadest issues relating to the corporation. These typically include changes of corporate name, address, purpose, the amount or type of shares, and other matters involving the corporate structure. Stockholders' action may also be needed on major legal or financial issues, such as whether to mortgage, encumber, pledge or lease all or substantially all of the corporate assets or to file bankruptcy, merge or consolidate. There are, of course, many other actions that can be taken by stockholders.

note The primary function of the stockholders, however, is to elect the board of directors, through whose governance the corporation is actually managed.

Stockholders can act officially only as a group. This means that a formal meeting is needed before they can legally bind the corporation. There are some exceptions where the stockholders can consent in writing to a particular action without having to hold a meeting. These instances, however, are rare.

Certain rules and procedures have to be followed for stockholders to properly conduct an official stockholder meeting:

1) Every stockholder has to be properly notified about the time and place of the meeting, who is calling the meeting, and any matters that will be considered at the meeting.

   It is common in small corporations for the stockholders to do without a formal notice, especially when the bylaws set the time and place of the regular annual meeting of stockholders. This can be done by having all the stockholders sign a waiver of notice at the meeting. Unscheduled or special meetings of stockholders may require notice, although a signed waiver of notice can also be used at these meetings. For an unscheduled meeting to be legally convened, it is essential that the records show that proper notice was given, or that the stockholders signed a waiver of notice.

Your Articles of Incorporation or bylaws will specify where and when a stockholder meeting can legally be held; the book of minutes should show the time and place of each meeting. In this way, you can prove that the meeting complied with the legal requirements.

2) No business can be transacted at a stockholders' meeting unless a quorum is present. Therefore, it is essential that the book of minutes reflect that a quorum of stockholders attended the meeting.

The bylaws or Articles of Incorporation will usually state the size of the quorum, either in terms of the number of stockholders or the number of shares that must be represented at the meeting. For example, a bylaw that "two-thirds of all stockholders shall constitute a quorum" applies to the number of stockholders, and not to the amount of the stock they own. On the other hand, a bylaw that states "a majority of the outstanding stock shall constitute a quorum" means that a certain number of shares of stock must be represented, regardless of whether the stock is owned by one person or by thousands of people.

> *note* If there is no rule on a quorum, then whatever number of stockholders shows up for the meeting will constitute a quorum.

3) Stockholder meetings must have a chairperson to preside over the meeting. They must also have a secretary to record what happens. The bylaws will ordinarily designate these officials by specifying that the president serve as chairperson and the secretary act as secretary; however, substitutes are usually allowable.

4) The first item of business at every stockholder meeting should be to approve the minutes of the previous meeting. Once the minutes are approved, they formally and legally document what occurred at the meeting. That is why it is important to show that the minutes have been approved as accurate, or that necessary changes have been made.

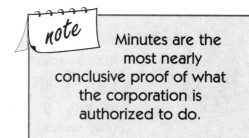

note Minutes are the most nearly conclusive proof of what the corporation is authorized to do.

5) Parliamentary procedure governs the conduct of meetings. It is not generally necessary to identify the person making the motion or seconding a motion, nor is it essential to record the exact tally of votes, as long as the action approved is clear.

Records of director actions

Most of the rules and procedures that apply to stockholder meetings apply equally to meetings of the board of directors with these exceptions:

- Directors will meet far more often than stockholders; in large corporations they may meet monthly. The directors can also hold special meetings for interim board action; in more active corporations they will routinely meet more often.

CAUTION Directors who may be in conflict with the interests of the corporation may not be counted toward the quorum, nor be entitled to vote.

- As with stockholders, the board can function only through a duly called meeting where a quorum of directors (as defined in the bylaws) is present.

- The board must be particularly careful to document not only its actions but why the action was taken. Because the board has responsibility to stockholders and potential liability to other constituencies, it may be called upon to show why its action was prudent, particularly in areas of dividends, loans to officers, compensation, contracts, and policy-making.

note It is especially critical for the minutes to include or refer to reports, arguments, opinions and other documents to support the reasonableness of the board's actions.

Many additional forms that allow the corporate board of directors to act on a wide variety of matters are available in Made E-Z Products' *Corporate Record Keeping Made E-Z*. Properly used, the forms in this guide will provide you with a simple, easy-to-use and legally sound records system for your corporation.

Dissolving your corporation

12

Chapter 12

Dissolving your corporation

Ten ways to dissolve a corporation

At some point, you may believe it is necessary to dissolve your corporation. There are many ways to do this, depending upon state law. A corporation may be dissolved by:

1) *Expiration.* The period specified in the corporate charter (Certificate of Incorporation) if any expiration date is stated.

2) *A surrender of the charter.* When the shareholders of a corporation, by majority vote, surrender the corporate charter to the state and it is formally accepted, the corporation is dissolved.

3) *Filing a Certificate of Dissolution.* File with the secretary of state in the state of incorporation.

4) *Consolidation.* When corporation A unites with corporation B to form a third but entirely separate corporation C, corporations A and B cease to exist and are said to have been dissolved "by consolidation." The new corporation C assumes all the assets, property rights, privileges and liabilities of former corporations A and B.

5) *Merger.* When corporation A merges into corporation B, only corporation A is dissolved "by merger." Corporation B survives. The surviving corporation absorbs all the assets, property rights, privileges, and often the liabilities of the absorbed corporation, but continues its own separate corporate existence thereafter.

6) *The occurrence of a condition.* A corporation may be dissolved when a condition (a specific event) clearly specified in the corporate charter occurs, such as the death of a principal. This provision is rare, however, as corporations have a perpetual life independent of their principals.

7) *Legislative repeal.* Under the inherent rights reserved by most states to "alter, amend, or repeal" the charter granted to a corporation, a legislature may, for some reason, find it necessary to revoke a corporate charter, thereby terminating the corporate existence. This is more commonly exercised with non-profit corporations.

8) *Action by the attorney general.* The state (and only the state) can sue to terminate the existence of a corporation. And if satisfied that the state has proven its case (e.g. when the court finds a corporation has not filed required taxes or documents or that it has abused or neglected to use its powers), the court may revoke the corporate charter.

9) *Directors' or shareholders' petition.* The board of directors (or a majority thereof) may be empowered by statute to petition for the

dissolution of a corporation upon the occurrence of certain events, e.g. when the assets of the corporation are not sufficient to discharge its liabilities. The stockholders of a majority of all outstanding shares entitled to vote on the issue may also be empowered by statute to make such petition to the court on similar grounds.

10) *Shareholders' petition under deadlock statutes.* A typical so-called "deadlock statute" commonly provides: "Unless otherwise provided in the Certificate of Incorporation, the holders of one-half of all outstanding shares of a corporation entitled to vote in an election of directors may present a petition for dissolution on one or more of the following grounds:

- That the directors are so divided respecting the management of the corporation's affairs that the votes required for action by the board cannot be obtained.

> *note* The dissolution of a corporation carries with it important tax and liability questions. Therefore dissolution should be undertaken only after consulting with an attorney and accountant.

- That the shareholders are so divided that the votes required for the election of directors cannot be obtained.

- That there is internal dissension and two or more factions of shareholders are so divided that dissolution would be beneficial to the shareholders."

Keep in mind that corporate dissolution is *not* the same as revocation of S corporation status, because the corporation continues to exist as a C corporation. If the corporation is dissolved, however, it reverts to proprietorship or partnership status.

The forms in this guide

MINUTE BOOK

———

- Bylaws

- Minutes

- Notices and Waivers

- Special Resolutions

- Stock Certificates and Register

Insert Here

a copy of your filed

Articles/Certificate of Incorporation

108

Bylaws

of

_____

adopted_____

BYLAWS
OF

_____

ARTICLE I
OFFICES

The principal office of the Corporation in the State of   shall be located in   , County of   . The Corporation may have such other offices, either within or without the State of   , as the Board of Directors may designate or as the business of the Corporation may require from time to time.

ARTICLE II
SHAREHOLDERS

SECTION 1. <u>Annual Meeting</u>. The annual meeting of the shareholders shall be held on the day in the month of   in each year, beginning with the year   , at the hour of   o'clock   .m., for the purpose of electing Directors and for the transaction of such other business as may come before the meeting. If the day fixed for the annual meeting shall be a legal holiday in the State of   , such meeting shall be held on the next succeeding business day. If the election of Directors shall not be held on the day designated herein for any annual meeting of the shareholders, or at any adjournment thereof, the Board of Directors shall cause the election to be held at a special meeting of the shareholders as soon thereafter as conveniently may be.

SECTION 2. <u>Special Meetings</u>. Special meetings of the shareholders, for any purpose or purposes, unless otherwise prescribed by statute, may be called by the President or by the Board of Directors, and shall be called by the President at the request of the holders of not less than   percent (%) of all the outstanding shares of the Corporation entitled to vote at the meeting.

SECTION 3. <u>Place of Meeting</u>. The Board of Directors may designate any place, either within or without the State of   , unless otherwise prescribed by statute, as the place of meeting for any annual meeting or for any special meeting. A waiver of notice signed by all shareholders entitled to vote at a meeting may designate any place, either within or without the State of   , unless otherwise prescribed by statute, as the place for the holding of such meeting. If no designation is made, the place of meeting shall be the principal office of the Corporation.

SECTION 4. <u>Notice of Meeting</u>. Written notice stating the place, day and hour of the meeting and, in case of a special meeting, the purpose or purposes for which the meeting is called, shall unless otherwise prescribed by statute, be delivered not less than   (   ) nor more than   (   ) days before the date of the meeting, to each shareholder of record entitled to vote at such meeting. If mailed, such notice shall be deemed to be delivered when deposited in the United States mail, addressed to the shareholder at his/her address as it appears on the stock transfer books of the Corporation, with postage thereon prepaid.

SECTION 5. <u>Closing of Transfer Books or Fixing of Record</u>. For the purpose of determining shareholders entitled to notice of or to vote at any meeting of shareholders or any adjournment thereof, or shareholders entitled to receive payment of any dividend, or in order to make a determination of share-holders for any other proper purpose, the Board of Directors of the Corporation may provide that the stock transfer books shall be closed for a stated period, but not to exceed in any case fifty (50) days. If the stock transfer books shall be closed for the purpose of determining shareholders entitled to notice of or to vote at a meeting of shareholders, such books shall be closed for at least (   ) days immediately preceding such meeting. In lieu of closing the stock transfer books, the Board of Directors may fix in advance a date as the record date for any such determination of share-holders, such date in any case to be not more than (   ) days and, in case of a meeting of shareholders, not less than (   ) days, prior to the date on which the particular action requiring such determination of shareholders is to be taken. If the stock transfer books are not closed and no record date is fixed for the determination of shareholders entitled to notice of or to vote at a meeting of shareholders, or shareholders entitled to receive payment of a dividend, the date on which notice of the meeting is mailed or the date on which the resolution of the Board of Directors declaring such dividend is adopted, as the case may be, shall be the record date for such determination of shareholders. When a determination of shareholders entitled to vote at any meeting of shareholders has been made as provided in this section, such determination shall apply to any adjournment thereof.

SECTION 6. <u>Voting Lists</u>. The officer or agent having charge of the stock transfer books for shares of the corporation shall make a complete list of the shareholders entitled to vote at each meeting of shareholders or any adjournment thereof, arranged in alphabetical order, with the address of and the number of shares held by each. Such list shall be produced and kept open at the time and place of the meeting and shall be subject to the inspection of any shareholder during the whole time of the meeting for the purposes thereof.

SECTION 7. <u>Quorum</u>. A majority of the outstanding shares of the Corporation entitled to vote, represented in person or by proxy, shall constitute a quorum at a meeting of shareholders. If less than a majority of the outstanding shares are represented at a meeting, a majority of the shares so represented may adjourn the meeting from time to time without further notice. At such adjourned meeting at which a quorum shall be present or represented, any business may be transacted which might have been trans-acted at the meeting as originally noticed. The shareholders present at a duly organized meeting may con-tinue to transact business until adjournment, notwithstanding the withdrawal of enough shareholders to leave less than a quorum.

SECTION 8. <u>Proxies</u>. At all meetings of shareholders, a shareholder may vote in person or by proxy executed in writing by the shareholder or by his/her duly authorized attorney-in-fact. Such proxy shall be filed with the secretary of the Corporation before or at the time of the meeting. A meeting of the Board of Directors may be had by means of a telephone conference or similar communications equip-ment by which all persons participating in the meeting can hear each other, and participation in a meet-ing under such circumstances shall constitute presence at the meeting.

SECTION 9. <u>Voting of Shares</u>. Each outstanding share entitled to vote shall be entitled to one vote upon each matter submitted to a vote at a meeting of shareholders.

SECTION 10. <u>Voting of Shares by Certain Holders</u>. Shares standing in the name of another corporation may be voted by such officer, agent or proxy as the Bylaws of such corporation may prescribe or, in the absence of such provision, as the Board of Directors of such corporation may determine. Shares held by an administrator, executor, guardian or conservator may be voted by him, either in person or by proxy, without a transfer of such shares into his name. Shares standing in the name of a trustee may be voted by him, either in person or by proxy, but no trustee shall be entitled to vote shares held by him without a transfer of such shares into his name.

Shares standing in the name of a receiver may be voted by such receiver, and shares held by or under the control of a receiver may be voted by such receiver without the transfer thereof into his name, if authority so to do be contained in an appropriate order of the court by which such receiver was appointed.

A shareholder whose shares are pledged shall be entitled to vote such shares until the shares have been transferred into the name of the pledgee, and thereafter the pledgee shall be entitled to vote the shares so transferred.

Shares of its own stock belonging to the Corporation shall not be voted, directly or indirectly, at any meeting, and shall not be counted in determining the total number of outstanding shares at any given time.

SECTION 11. <u>Informal Action by Shareholders</u>. Unless otherwise provided by law, any action required to be taken at a meeting of the shareholders, or any other action which may be taken at a meeting of the shareholders, may be taken without a meeting if a consent in writing, setting forth the action so taken, shall be signed by all of the shareholders entitled to vote with respect to the subject matter thereof.

ARTICLE III
BOARD OF DIRECTORS

SECTION 1. <u>General Powers</u>. The business and affairs of the Corporation shall be managed by its Board of Directors.

SECTION 2. <u>Number, Tenure and Qualifications</u>. The number of directors of the Corporation shall be fixed by the Board of Directors, but in no event shall be less than (   ). Each director shall hold office until the next annual meeting of shareholders and until his/her successor shall have been elected and qualified.

SECTION 3. <u>Regular Meetings</u>. A regular meeting of the Board of Directors shall be held without other notice than this Bylaw immediately after, and at the same place as, the annual meeting of shareholders. The Board of Directors may provide, by resolution, the time and place for the holding of additional regular meetings without notice other than such resolution.

SECTION 4. <u>Special Meetings</u>. Special meetings of the Board of Directors may be called by or at the request of the President or any two directors. The person or persons authorized to call special meetings of the Board of Directors may fix the place for holding any special meeting of the Board of Directors called by them.

SECTION 5. <u>Notice</u>. Notice of any special meeting shall be given at least one (1) day previous thereto by written notice delivered personally or mailed to each director at his business address, or by telegram. If mailed, such notice shall be deemed to be delivered when deposited in the United States mail so addressed, with postage thereon prepaid. If notice be given by telegram, such notice shall be deemed to be delivered when the telegram is delivered to the telegraph company. Any directors may waive notice of any meeting. The attendance of a director at a meeting shall constitute a waiver of notice of such meeting, except where a director attends a meeting for the express purpose of objecting to the transaction of any business because the meeting is not lawfully called or convened.

SECTION 6. Quorum. A majority of the number of directors fixed by Section 2 of this Article III shall constitute a quorum for the transaction of business at any meeting of the Board of Directors, but if less than such majority is present at a meeting, a majority of the directors present may adjourn the meeting from time to time without further notice.

SECTION 7. Manner of Acting. The act of the majority of the directors present at a meeting at which a quorum is present shall be the act of the Board of Directors.

SECTION 8. Action Without a Meeting. Any action that may be taken by the Board of Directors at a meeting may be taken without a meeting if a consent in writing, setting forth the action so to be taken, shall be signed before such action by all of the directors.

SECTION 9. Vacancies. Any vacancy occurring in the Board of Directors may be filled by the affirmative vote of a majority of the remaining directors though less than a quorum of the Board of Directors, unless otherwise provided by law. A director elected to fill a vacancy shall be elected for the unexpired term of his/her predecessor in office. Any directorship to be filled by reason of an increase in the number of directors may be filled by election by the Board of Directors for a term of office continuing only until the next election of directors by the shareholders.

SECTION 10. Compensation. By resolution of the Board of Directors, each director may be paid his/her expenses, if any, of attendance at each meeting of the Board of Directors, and may be paid a stated salary as director or a fixed sum for attendance at each meeting of the Board of Directors or both. No such payment shall preclude any director from serving the Corporation in any other capacity and receiving compensation therefor.

SECTION 11. Presumption of Assent. A director of the Corporation who is present at a meeting of the Board of Directors at which action on any corporate matter is taken shall be presumed to have assented to the action taken unless his/her dissent shall be entered in the minutes of the meeting or unless he/she shall file written dissent to such action with the person acting as the Secretary of the meeting before the adjournment thereof, or shall forward such dissent by registered mail to the Secretary of the Corporation immediately after the adjournment of the meeting. Such right to dissent shall not apply to a director who voted in favor of such action.

ARTICLE IV
OFFICERS

SECTION 1. Number. The officers of the Corporation shall be a President, one or more Vice Presidents, a Secretary and a Treasurer, each of whom shall be elected by the Board of Directors. Such other officers and assistant officers as may be deemed necessary may be elected or appointed by the Board of Directors, including a Chairman of the Board. In its discretion, the Board of Directors may leave unfilled for any such period as it may determine any office except those of President and Secretary. Any two or more offices may be held by the same person, except for the offices of President and Secretary which may not be held by the same person. Officers may be directors or shareholders of the Corporation.

SECTION 2. Election and Term of Office. The officers of the Corporation to be elected by the Board of Directors shall be elected annually by the Board of Directors at the first meeting of the Board of Directors held after each annual meeting of the shareholders. If the election of officers shall not be held at such meeting, such election shall be held as soon thereafter as conveniently may be. Each officer shall hold office until his/her successor shall have been duly elected and shall have qualified, or until his/her death, or until he/she shall resign or shall have been removed in the manner hereinafter provided.

SECTION 3. Removal. Any officer or agent may be removed by the Board of Directors whenever, in its judgement, the best interests of the Corporation will be served thereby, but such removal shall be without prejudice to the contract rights, if any, of the person so removed. Election or appointment of an officer or agent shall not of itself create contract rights, and such appointment shall be terminable at will.

SECTION 4. Vacancies. A vacancy in any office because of death, resignation, removal, disqualification or otherwise, may be filled by the Board of Directors for the unexpired portion of the term.

SECTION 5. President. The President shall be the principal executive officer of the Corporation and, subject to the control of the Board of Directors, shall in general supervise and control all of the business and affairs of the Corporation. He/she shall, when present, preside at all meetings of the shareholders and of the Board of Directors, unless there is a Chairman of the Board, in which case the Chairman shall preside. The President may sign, with the Secretary or any other proper officer of the Corporation thereunto authorized by the Board of Directors, certificates for shares of the Corporation, any deeds, mortgages, bonds, contracts, or other instruments which the Board of Directors has authorized to be executed, except in cases where the signing and execution thereof shall be expressly delegated by the Board of Directors or by these Bylaws to some other officer or agent of the Corporation, or shall be required by law to be otherwise signed or executed; and in general shall perform all duties incident to the office of President and such other duties as may be prescribed by the Board of Directors from time to time.

SECTION 6. Vice President. In the absence of the President or in event of his/her death, inability or refusal to act, the Vice President shall perform the duties of the President, and when so acting, shall have all the powers of and be subject to all the restrictions upon the President. The Vice President shall perform such other duties as from time to time may be assigned by the President or by the Board of Directors. If there is more than one Vice President, each Vice President shall succeed to the duties of the President in order of rank as determined by the Board of Directors. If no such rank has been determined, then each Vice President shall succeed to the duties of the President in order of date of election, the earliest date having the first rank.

SECTION 7. Secretary. The Secretary shall: (a) keep the minutes of the proceedings of the shareholders and of the Board of Directors in one or more minute books provided for that purpose; (b) see that all notices are duly given in accordance with the provisions of these Bylaws or as required by law; (c) be custodian of the corporate records and of the seal of the Corporation and see that the seal of the Corporation is affixed to all documents, the execution of which on behalf of the Corporation under its seal is duly authorized; (d) keep a register of the post office address of each shareholder which shall be furnished to the Secretary by such shareholder; (e) sign with the President certificates for shares of the Corporation, the issuance of which shall have been authorized by resolution of the Board of Directors; (f) have general charge of the stock transfer books of the Corporation; and (g) in general perform all duties incident to the office of the Secretary and such other duties as from time to time may be assigned by the President or by the Board of Directors.

SECTION 8. Treasurer. The Treasurer shall: (a) have charge and custody of and be responsible for all funds and securities of the Corporation; (b) receive and give receipts for moneys due and payable to the Corporation from any source whatsoever, and deposit all such moneys in the name of the Corporation in such banks, trust companies or other depositories as shall be selected in accordance with the provisions of Article VI of these Bylaws; and (c) in general perform all of the duties incident to the office of Treasurer and such other duties as from time to time may be assigned to him by the President or by the Board of Directors. If required by the Board of Directors, the Treasurer shall give a bond for the faithful discharge of his/her duties in such sum and with such sureties as the Board of Directors shall determine.

SECTION 9. Salaries. The salaries of the officers shall be fixed from time to time by the Board of Directors, and no officer shall be prevented from receiving such salary by reason of the fact that he/she is also a director of the Corporation.

ARTICLE V
INDEMNITY

The Corporation shall indemnify its directors, officers and employees as follows:

(a) Every director, officer, or employee of the Corporation shall be indemnified by the Corporation against all expenses and liabilities, including counsel fees, reasonably incurred by or imposed upon him/her in connection with any proceeding to which he/she may be made a party, or in which he/she may become involved, by reason of being or having been a director, officer, employee or agent of the Corporation or is or was serving at the request of the Corporation as a director, officer, employee or agent of the corporation, partnership, joint venture, trust or enterprise, or any settlement thereof, whether or not he/she is a director, officer, employee or agent at the time such expenses are incurred, except in such cases wherein the director, officer, or employee is adjudged guilty of willful mis-feasance or malfeasance in the performance of his/her duties; provided that in the event of a settlement the indemnification herein shall apply only when the Board of Directors approves such settlement and reimbursement as being for the best interests of the Corporation.

(b) The Corporation shall provide to any person who is or was a director, officer, employee, or agent of the Corporation or is or was serving at the request of the Corporation as a director, officer, employee or agent of the corporation, partnership, joint venture, trust or enterprise, the indemnity against expenses of suit, litigation or other proceedings which is specifically permissible under applicable law.

(c) The Board of Directors may, in its discretion, direct the purchase of liability insurance by way of implementing the provisions of this Article V.

ARTICLE VI
CONTRACTS, LOANS, CHECKS AND DEPOSITS

SECTION 1. Contracts. The Board of Directors may authorize any officer or officers, agent or agents, to enter into any contract or execute and deliver any instrument in the name of and on behalf of the Corporation, and such authority may be general or confined to specific instances.

SECTION 2. Loans. No loans shall be contracted on behalf of the Corporation and no evidences of indebtedness shall be issued in its name unless authorized by a resolution of the Board of Directors. Such authority may be general or confined to specific instances.

SECTION 3. Checks, Drafts, etc. All checks, drafts or other orders for the payment of money, notes or other evidences of indebtedness issued in the name of the Corporation, shall be signed by such officer or officers, agent or agents of the Corporation and in such manner as shall from time to time be determined by resolution of the Board of Directors.

SECTION 4. Deposits. All funds of the Corporation not otherwise employed shall be deposited from time to time to the credit of the Corporation in such banks, trust companies or other depositories as the Board of Directors may select.

ARTICLE VII
CERTIFICATES FOR SHARES AND THEIR TRANSFER

SECTION 1. Certificates for Shares. Certificates representing shares of the Corporation shall be in such form as shall be determined by the Board of Directors. Such certificates shall be signed by the President and by the Secretary or by such other officers authorized by law and by the Board of Directors so to do, and sealed with the corporate seal. All certificates for shares shall be consecutively numbered or otherwise identified. The name and address of the person to whom the shares represented thereby are issued, with the number of shares and date of issue, shall be entered on the stock transfer books of the Corporation. All certificates surrendered to the Corporation for transfer shall be cancelled and no new certificate shall be issued until the former certificate for a like number of shares shall have been surrendered and cancelled, except that in case of a lost, destroyed or mutilated certificate, a new one may be issued therefor upon such terms and indemnity to the Corporation as the Board of Directors may prescribe.

SECTION 2. Transfer of Shares. Transfer of shares of the Corporation shall be made only on the stock transfer books of the Corporation by the holder of record thereof or by his/her legal representative, who shall furnish proper evidence of authority to transfer, or by his/her attorney thereunto authorized by power of attorney duly executed and filed with the Secretary of the Corporation, and on surrender for cancellation of the certificate for such shares. The person in whose name shares stand on the books of the Corporation shall be deemed by the Corporation to be the owner thereof for all purposes. Provided, however, that upon any action undertaken by the shareholders to elect S Corporation status pursuant to Section 1362 of the Internal Revenue Code and upon any shareholders' agreement thereto restricting the transfer of said shares so as to disqualify said S Corporation status, said restriction on transfer shall be made a part of the bylaws so long as said agreement is in force and effect.

ARTICLE VIII
FISCAL YEAR

The fiscal year of the Corporation shall begin on the   day of   and end on the day of   of each year.

ARTICLE IX
DIVIDENDS

The Board of Directors may from time to time declare, and the Corporation may pay, dividends on its outstanding shares in the manner and upon the terms and conditions provided by law and its Articles of Incorporation.

ARTICLE X
CORPORATE SEAL

The Board of Directors shall provide a corporate seal which shall be circular in form and shall have inscribed thereon the name of the Corporation and the state of incorporation and the words, "Corporate Seal."

ARTICLE XI
WAIVER OF NOTICE

Unless otherwise provided by law, whenever any notice is required to be given to any shareholder or director of the Corporation under the provisions of these Bylaws or under the provisions of the Articles of Incorporation or under the provisions of the applicable Business Corporation Act, a waiver thereof in writing, signed by the person or persons entitled to such notice, whether before or after the time stated therein, shall be deemed equivalent to the giving of such notice.

ARTICLE XII
AMENDMENTS

These Bylaws may be altered, amended or repealed and new Bylaws may be adopted by the Board of Directors at any regular or special meeting of the Board of Directors.

The above Bylaws are certified to have been adopted by the Board of Directors of the Corporation on the _____ day of _____ , _____ (year).

_____
Secretary

WAIVER OF NOTICE OF MEETING
OF INCORPORATORS AND DIRECTORS OF

_____

We the undersigned do hereby constitute all the incorporators and directors of the above-named corporation and do hereby waive notice as to time and place of the first meeting of incorporators and directors of the aforesaid corporation.

Furthermore, we hereby consent and agree that said meeting shall be held at   o'clock .m. on   ,   (year) at the following place:

_____

We do hereby affix our names to show our waiver of notice of said meeting.

_____   _____

_____   _____

_____   _____

_____   _____

Dated:

NOTICE OF ORGANIZATION MEETING
OF INCORPORATORS AND DIRECTORS

TO: _____

     _____

     _____

PLEASE BE ADVISED THAT:

We, the undersigned, do hereby constitute a majority of the directors named in the Articles of Incorporation of _____, a corporation;

Pursuant to state law, we are hereby calling an organization meeting of the Board of Directors and incorporators named in the Articles of Incorporation of the above named corporation for the purpose of adopting bylaws, electing officers, and transacting such other business as may come before the meeting; and

Said organization meeting shall be held at_____

_____ on

_____ , _____ (year), at _____ o'clock _____ .m.

_____   _____

_____   _____

_____   _____

_____   _____

RECEIPT OF NOTICE

_____   _____
       Addressee-Director   Date Received

MINUTES OF ORGANIZATION MEETING
OF BOARD OF DIRECTORS OF

_____

The organizational meeting of the Board of Directors of
was held at
on   ,   (year), at   .m. Present were:

_____   _____

_____   _____

_____   _____

being persons designated as the Directors in the Articles of Incorporation.

Absent from the meeting were:

_____   _____

_____   _____

_____   _____

acted as temporary Chairman of the meeting and
acted as temporary Secretary.

The Chairman announced that the meeting had been duly called by the Incorporators of the Corporation.

The Chairman reported that the Articles of Incorporation of the Corporation had been duly filed with the State of   on   ,   (year). The Certificate of Incorporation and a copy of said Articles of Incorporation were ordered to be inserted in the Minutes as a part of the records of the meeting.

A proposed form of Bylaws for the regulation and the management of the affairs of the Corporation was then presented at the meeting. The Bylaws were read and considered and, upon motion duly made and seconded, it was:

RESOLVED, that the form of Bylaws of the Corporation, as presented to this meeting, a copy of which is directed to be inserted in the Minute Book of the Corporation be, and the same are hereby approved and adopted as, the Bylaws of the Corporation.

The following persons were nominated officers of the Corporation to serve until their respective successors are chosen and qualify:

PRESIDENT:
VICE PRESIDENT:
SECRETARY:
TREASURER:

The Chairman announced that the aforenamed persons had been elected to the office set opposite their respective names.

The President thereupon took the chair and the Secretary immediately assumed the discharge of the duties of that office.

The President then stated that there were a number of organizational matters to be considered at the meeting and a number of resolutions to be adopted by the Board of Directors.

The form of stock certificates was then exhibited at the meeting. Thereupon, a motion duly made and seconded, it was:

RESOLVED, that the form of stock certificates presented at this meeting be, and the same is hereby adopted and approved as, the stock certificate of the Corporation, a specimen copy of the stock certificate to be inserted with these Minutes.

FURTHER RESOLVED, that the officers are hereby authorized to pay or reimburse the payment of all fees and expenses incident to and necessary for the organization of this Corporation.

The Board of Directors then considered the opening of a corporate bank account to serve as a depository for the funds of the Corporation. Following discussion, on motion duly made and seconded, it was:

RESOLVED, that the Treasurer be authorized, empowered and directed to open an account with and to deposit all funds of the Corporation, all drafts, checks and notes of the Corporation, payable on said account to be made in the corporate name signed by

.

FURTHER RESOLVED, that officers are hereby authorized to execute such resolutions (including formal Bank Resolutions), documents and other instruments as may be necessary or advisable in opening or continuing said bank account. A copy of the applicable printed form of Bank Resolution hereby adopted to supplement these Minutes is ordered appended to the Minutes of this meeting.

It is announced that the following persons have offered to transfer the property listed below in exchange for the following shares of the stock of the Corporation:

Name	Payment Consideration, or Property	Number of Shares

Upon motion duly made and seconded, it was:

RESOLVED, that acceptance of the offer of the above-named stock subscribers is in the best interest of the Corporation and necessary for carrying out the corporate business, and in the judgment of the Board of Directors, the assets proposed to be transferred to the Corporation are reasonably worth the amount of consideration deemed therefor, and the same hereby is accepted, and that upon receipt of the consideration indicated above, the President and the Secretary are authorized to issue certificates of fully-paid, non-assessable capital stock of this Corporation in the amounts indicated to the above-named persons.

In order to provide for the payment of expenses of incorporation and organization of the Corporation, on motion duly made, seconded and unanimously carried, the following resolution was adopted:

RESOLVED, that the President and the Secretary and/or Treasurer of this Corporation be and they are hereby authorized and directed to pay the expenses of this Corporation, including attorney's fees for incorporation, and to reimburse the persons who have made disbursements thereof.

After consideration of the pertinent issues with regard to the tax year and accounting basis, on motion duly made, and seconded and unanimously carried, the following resolution was adopted:

RESOLVED, that the first fiscal year of the Corporation shall commence on   , and end on   .

FURTHER RESOLVED, that the President be and is hereby authorized and directed to enter into employment contracts with certain employees, such contract shall be for the term and the rate stated in the attached Employment Agreements.

FURTHER RESOLVED, that it shall be the policy of the Corporation to reimburse each employee or to pay directly on his behalf all expenses incidental to his attendance at conventions and seminars as may be approved by the President. Reimbursement shall include full reimbursement for commercial and private transportation expenses, plus other necessary and ordinary out-of-pocket expenses incidental to the said travel, including meals and lodging.

A general discussion was then held concerning the immediate commencement of business operations as a Corporation and it was determined that business operations of the Corporation would commence as of   . It was agreed that no fixed date would be set for holding meetings of the Board of Directors except the regular meetings to be held immediately after the annual meetings of shareholders as provided in the Bylaws of the Corporation, but that meetings of the Directors would be periodically called by the President and Secretary or others as provided by the Bylaws. Upon motion duly made, seconded and unanimously carried, it was:

RESOLVED, that the officers of the Corporation are hereby authorized to do any and all things necessary to conduct the business of the Corporation as set forth in the Articles of Incorporation and Bylaws of the Corporation.

Upon motion duly made, seconded, and unanimously carried the following resolution was adopted:

RESOLVED, that, if required,   be, and hereby is, appointed Resident Agent in the State of   .

The office of the Resident Agent will be located at

.

The Chairman then presented to the meeting the question of electing the provisions of Section 1244 of the Internal Revenue Code. He noted that this Section permits ordinary loss treatment when either the holder of Section 1244 stock sells or exchanges such stock at a loss or when such stock becomes worthless. After a discussion, the following preamble was stated and the following resolution was unanimously:

RESOLVED, THAT:

WHEREAS, this Corporation qualifies as a small business corporation as defined in Section 1244, but

WHEREAS, the Board of Directors is concerned over future tax law changes modifying Section 1244 as presently enacted (subsequent to the Revenue Act of 1978) and thus desires to safeguard this Corporation's 1244 election by complying with prior law as well as present law, and

WHEREAS, pursuant to the requirements of Section 1244 and the Regulations issued thereunder, the following plan has been submitted to the Corporation by the Board of Directors of the Corporation:

(a) The plan as hereafter set forth shall, upon its adoption by the Board of Directors of the Corporation, immediately become effective.

(b) No more than   shares of common stock are authorized to be issued under this plan, such stock to have a par value of $ per share.

(c) Stock authorized under this plan shall be issued only in exchange for money, or property susceptible to monetary valuation other than capital stock, securities or services rendered or to be rendered. The aggregate dollar amount to be received for such stock shall not exceed $1,000,000, and the sum of each aggregate dollar amount and the equity capital of the Corporation (determined on the date of adoption of the plan) shall not exceed $1,000,000.

(d) Any stock options granted during the life of this plan which apply to the stock issuable hereunder shall apply solely to such stock and to no other and must be exercised within the period in which the plan is effective.

(e) Such other action as may be necessary shall be taken by the Corporation to qualify the stock to be offered and issued under this plan as "Section 1244 Stock," as such term is defined in the Internal Revenue Code and the regulations issued thereunder.

NOW, THEREFORE, the foregoing plan to issue Section 1244 Stock is adopted by the Corporation and the appropriate officers of the Corporation are authorized and directed to take all actions deemed by them necessary to carry out the intent and purpose of the recited plan.

There being no further business requiring Board action or consideration, on motion duly made, seconded and carried, the meeting was adjourned.

Dated:

_____
Secretary of the Meeting

WAIVER OF NOTICE,
FIRST MEETING OF SHAREHOLDERS

We the undersigned, being the shareholders of the
, agree that the first meeting of shareholders be on the date and at the time
and place stated below in order to elect officers and transact such other business as may lawfully come
before the meeting. We hereby waive all notice of such meeting and of any adjournment thereof.

Place of Meeting:_____

Date of Meeting:_____

Time of Meeting:_____

_____

_____

_____

_____

Dated:_____   _____
                                 Shareholders

MINUTES, FIRST MEETING
OF SHAREHOLDERS

The first meeting of the shareholders of
was held at
on the   day of   ,   (year), at   . m.

The meeting was duly called to order by the President, who stated the purpose of the meeting.

Next, the Secretary read the list of shareholders as they appear in the record book of the Corporation and reported the presence of a quorum of shareholders.

Next, the Secretary read a waiver of notice of the meeting, signed by all shareholders. On a motion duly made, seconded and carried, the waiver was ordered appended to the minutes of this meeting.

Next, the President asked the Secretary to read:

(1) the minutes of the organization meeting of the Corporation; and
(2) the minutes of the first meeting of the Board of Directors.

A motion was duly made, seconded and carried unanimously that the following resolution be adopted:

WHEREAS, the minutes of the organization meeting of the Corporation and the minutes of the first meeting of the Board of Directors have been read to this meeting, and

WHEREAS, bylaws were adopted and directors and officers were elected at the organization meeting, it is hereby

RESOLVED that this meeting approves and ratifies the election of the said directors and officers of this Corporation for the term of   years, and approves, ratifies and adopts said bylaws as the bylaws of the corporation. It is further

RESOLVED that all acts taken and decisions made at the organization meeting and the first meeting of the Board are approved and ratified. It is further

RESOLVED that signing of these minutes constitutes full ratification by the signatories and waiver of notice of the meeting.

There being no further business, the meeting was adjourned.

Dated the   day of   ,   (year).

_____
Secretary

_____   _____
Director   Director

_____   _____
Director   Director

Appended hereto: Waiver of notice of meeting.

126

MINUTES, SHAREHOLDERS' ANNUAL MEETING

The Annual Meeting of Shareholders of _____

was held at _____, State of _____, on the

_____ day of _____, _____ (year), at _____ o'clock, _____ .m.

The President duly called the meeting to order and outlined its purposes.

The Secretary next stated that a notice of meeting had been properly served, introducing an affidavit to this effect which was ordered placed on file. (OR: The Secretary stated that a waiver of notice of the meeting had been properly signed by the shareholders and it was placed on file.)

The President proposed the immediate election of a Chairman. A motion to that effect was duly made and carried.

It being determined that a quorum was present either in person or by proxy, a voice vote of shareholders was taken. _____ was elected Chairman of the meeting.

A motion was duly made and carried that the Secretary read the minutes of the preceding meeting of shareholders. Upon completion of the reading, a motion was duly made and carried that the minutes be approved as read. (OR: A motion was duly made and carried that a reading of the preceding meeting of shareholders be waived.)

The President then presented his/her annual report. (Include report.)

A motion was duly made, seconded and carried that the report be received and filed.

The Secretary next presented his/her report. (Include report.)

A motion was duly made, seconded and carried that the report be received and filed.

The Treasurer then presented his/her report. (Include report.)

A motion was duly made, seconded and carried that the report be received and filed.

The Chairman said that election of directors of the Corporation for the coming year was the next order of business.

The following were nominated as directors.

_____   _____

_____   _____

_____   _____

The Chairman then stated that the Board has appointed _____

_____and_____ as inspectors of election and that

they would receive and tally the ballots.

Each shareholder was asked to place his vote in a ballot, stating the number of shares voted,

and to sign his name.

The inspectors, after completing a tally of the vote, declared that the following votes had been

cast:

Names of Nominees   Number of Votes

_____   _____

_____   _____

_____   _____

_____   _____

_____   _____

The Chairman then announced that the following persons had been elected directors:

_____

_____.

A motion was duly made, seconded and carried that the inspectors file the report with the Clerk of

_____ County (when required by law) and the the Secretary of the

Corporation.

There being no further business, a motion was duly made, seconded and carried that the

meeting be adjourned.

Dated the _____ day of _____, _____(year).

                                    _____
                                    Secretary

NOTICE TO DIRECTORS
OF REGULAR BOARD MEETING

A meeting of the Board of _____ will be held at the office of

the Corporation at _____, City of_____,

State of _____, on the_____ day of _____, _____(year),

at _____ o'clock _____.m., for the purpose of transacting all such business as may properly come

before the same.

Dated the _____day of _____, _____(year).

_____
Secretary

MINUTES, REGULAR BOARD MEETING

A meeting of the Board was held at _____ on the _____day of _____, _____(year), at _____o'clock____.m.

The President called the meeting to order.

The Secretary called the roll. The following directors were present: _____, _____, _____.

The Secretary reported that notice of the time and place of holding the meeting had been given to each director by mail in accordance with the bylaws.

A motion was duly made, seconded and carried that the notice be filed.

The President then stated that, a quorum being present, the meeting could transact business.

Minutes of the preceding meeting of the Board, held _____, _____(year), were read and adopted.

The President presented his/her report.

A motion was made, seconded and carried that the President's report be filed.

A motion was made, seconded and carried, that _____ be appointed to audit the books of the Treasurer before the same are presented to the shareholders.

A motion was duly made and carried that the meeting elect officers for the ensuing year.

The following were thereupon elected by ballot:

President: _____

Vice-President: _____

Secretary: _____

Treasurer: _____

A motion was duly made and carried that salaries of officers be fixed as follows:

Name _____ Salary per year _____

Name _____ Salary per year _____

Name _____ Salary per year _____

There was no further business. The meeting was adjourned.

Dated: _____, _____(year)

_____
Secretary

MINUTES, DIRECTORS' MEETING

_____

A regular meeting of the Board of Directors of the Corporation was held at the office of the Corporation, at   , on   ,

(year), at   o'clock   .m.

There were present and participating at the meeting:

_____   _____

_____   _____

_____   _____

_____   _____

being a quorum of the directors of the Corporation.

               , President of the Corporation, acted as Chairman of the meeting, and   , Secretary of the Corporation, acted as Secretary of the meeting.

The Secretary presented notice or a waiver of notice of the meeting, signed by all the directors.

The meeting, having been duly convened, was ready to proceed with its business, whereupon it was:

RESOLVED, That the salary of   , as President of the Corporation, be fixed at   Dollars ($) per year.

RESOLVED, Further that the salary of   , as Vice President of the Corporation, be fixed at   Dollars ($) per year.

RESOLVED, Further that the salary of   , as Treasurer of the Corporation, be fixed at   Dollars ($) per year.

RESOLVED, Further that the salary of   , as Secretary of

the Corporation, be fixed at   Dollars ($) per year.

RESOLVED, That in addition to their present salaries, the officers of the Corporation,

comprising   ,   ,

                    , and   ,

holding, respectively, the offices of   ,

                        ,   , and

                    , shall participate in all fringe benefit programs available to employees

of the Corporation from time to time.

A True Record

Attest

_____

Chairman

_____

Secretary

ASSIGNMENT OF ASSETS

This agreement is made and entered into this   day of   ,   (year),

by and between

(Stockholder) and   , a Corporation hereinafter

referred to as "Corporation."

WITNESSETH:

WHEREAS, on the   day of   ,   (year), the Corporation will have

been formed by Articles of Incorporation being filed with the Secretary of State of

and at the time it was necessary to transfer certain assets into the Corporation in order to capitalize the

Corporation; and

WHEREAS,   is desirous of transferring to the Corporation

certain assets shown on the attached Exhibit "A", and the Corporation is desirous of receiving said assets,

NOW, THEREFORE, for and in consideration of the mutual covenants and agreements

hereinafter entered into, it is agreed as follows:

1.   does hereby transfer and assign those assets listed on the

attached Exhibit "A" to the Corporation.

2.   In consideration for said transfer, the Corporation issues to   ,

(   ) shares of   stock in the Corporation, par value

$ per share.

DATED this   day of   ,   (year).

_____
Stockholder

By: _____
      Corporation

MEDICAL CARE REIMBURSEMENT PLAN
OF

_____

FIRST: The Corporation shall reimburse all eligible employees for expenses incurred by themselves and their dependents, and defined in Internal Revenue Code, Section 152, as amended, for medical care, as defined in Internal Revenue Code, Section 213(3), as amended, subject to the conditions and limitations as hereinafter set forth. It is the intention of the Corporation that the benefits payable to eligible employees hereunder shall be excluded from their gross income pursuant to Internal Revenue Code, Section 105, as amended.

SECOND: All corporate officers employed on a full-time basis at the date of inception of this Plan, including those who may be absent due to illness or injury on said date, are eligible employees under the Plan. A corporate officer shall be considered employed on a full-time basis if said officer customarily works at least seven months in each year and twenty hours in each week. Any person hereafter becoming an officer of the Corporation employed on a full-time basis shall be eligible under this Plan.

THIRD: (a) The Corporation shall reimburse any eligible employee (check one) ___ without limitation ___ no more than $_____ in any fiscal year for medical care expenses, (b) Reimbursement or payment is not provided under any insurance policy(ies), whether owned by the Corporation or the employee, or under any health and accident or wage-continuation plan. In the event that there is such an insurance policy or plan in effect, providing for reimbursement in whole or in part, then to the extent of the coverage under such policy or plan, the Corporation shall be relieved of any liability hereunder.

FOURTH: Any eligible employee applying for reimbursement under this Plan shall submit to the Corporation, at least quarterly, all bills for medical care including premium notices for accident or health insurance, for verification by the Corporation prior to payment. Failure to comply herewith may, at the discretion of the Corporation, terminate such eligible employee's right to said reimbursement.

FIFTH: The Plan shall be subject to termination, at any time, by vote of the Board of Directors of the Corporation; provided, however, that medical care expenses incurred prior to such termination shall be reimbursed or paid in accordance with this Plan.

SIXTH: The President shall determine all questions arising from the administration and interpretation of the Plan except where reimbursement is claimed by the President. In such case, determination shall be made by the Board of Directors.

ADOPTED this   day of   ,   (year).

By: _____
                    President

_____
            Secretary

_____
    For the Board of Directors

RESOLUTION RATIFYING THE ANNEXED
MEDICAL CARE REIMBURSEMENT PLAN

Pursuant to the Bylaws of
          , a(n)   corporation, the undersigned, representing (check one) ___ all ___ a majority of the members of the Board of Directors of said corporation, hereby enact the following resolution:

RESOLVED, that the "Medical Care Reimbursement Plan" presented to this meeting is hereby approved and adopted; that a copy of the Plan is annexed to this Resolution; and that the proper Officers of the corporation are hereby authorized to take whatever action is necessary to implement the Plan.

AND IT IS FURTHER RESOLVED, that the signing of this Resolution by the directors shall constitute full ratification thereof.

RATIFIED this   day of   ,   (year).

_____   _____

_____   _____

_____   _____

_____   _____

NOTICE TO SHAREHOLDERS
OF ANNUAL MEETING

The Annual Meeting of Shareholders of _____

for the purpose of electing _____Directors, and transacting such other business as may

properly come before the meeting, will be held on the _____ day of _____,

_____(year), at _____ o'clock _____.m., at the office of _____

_____, City of _____ and State of _____.

Transfer books will remain closed from the _____day of _____,

_____(year), until the _____day of _____, _____(year).

Dated the _____ day of _____, _____(year).

_____

Secretary

STOCK LEDGER AND TRANSFER LEDGER

NAME AND ADDRESS OF STOCKHOLDERS	DATE ISSUED	NAME OF SECURITY	CERTIFICATE NUMBER	VALUE OF SHARES	DATE TRANSFERRED	CERTIFICATES TRANSFERRED	SHARES TRANSFERRED	BALANCE OF SHARES

STOCKHOLDER'S PROXY

KNOWN ALL BY THESE PRESENTS, that

, the undersigned,

being the owner(s) of   (   ) shares of Stock of   ,

a(n)   Corporation, do hereby constitute and appoint

, whose address is   , in the

City of   , State of   , my (our) true and lawful Attorney-In-Fact, for and in

my (our) name, place and stead, to vote upon the Stock owned by me (us), or standing in my (our) name,

as my (our) PROXY at the Meeting of the Stockholders of said Corporation, to be held at

, in the City of   ,

State of   on   ,   (year), at the hour of   o'clock

m., or such other day and time as the meeting may be thereafter held by adjournment or otherwise

according the number of votes now, or may then be entitled to be voted, hereby granting said Attorney-In-Fact full power and authority to act for me (us) and in my (our) name at the meeting or meetings in the

transaction of such other business as may come before the meeting, as fully as I (we) could do if person-

ally present, with full power of substitution and revocation, hereby ratifying and confirming all that my

(our) said Attorney-In-Fact or substitute may do in my (our) place, name and stead.

This Proxy is to continue in full force until   ,   (year), but

may be revoked at any time by notice thereof in writing, filed with the Secretary of the Corporation.

IN WITNESS WHEREOF, I (WE) have hereunto set my(our) hand(s) and seal this

day of   ,   (year).

_____   _____

STATE OF
COUNTY OF

On   before me,   ,

personally appeared

personally known to me (or proved to me on the basis of satisfactory evidence) to be the person(s) whose
name(s) is/are subscribed to the within instrument and acknowledged to me that he/she/they executed the
same in his/her/their authorized capacity(ies), and that by his/her/their signature(s) on the instrument the
person(s), or the entity upon behalf of which the person(s) acted, executed the instrument. WITNESS my
hand and official seal.

Signature_____   Affiant____Known____Produced ID
        Notary Public   ID Produced_____

                                                          (Seal)

CERTIFICATE OF INCORPORATION
OF

_____

We the undersigned, as proper persons acting as incorporators of a corporation under the laws of the State of New York, adopt this Certificate of Incorporation of _____

_____

and the following Articles of Incorporation under section 402 of the Business Corporation Law:

FIRST The name of the corporation is: _____.

SECOND The address of the principal place of business of the corporation (including county) is

_____

THIRD The period of its duration is: [perpetual] [if not perpetual, state period] _____

_____.

FOURTH The purpose of the corporation is: _____

_____

_____.

FIFTH The aggregate number of authorized shares is: _____.

SIXTH The shares [have no par value] [have a par value of] _____.

SEVENTH The corporation will not commence business until at least _____ dollars have been received by it as consideration for the issuance of shares.

EIGHTH Cumulative voting of shares of stock [is] [is not] authorized.

NINTH Provisions limiting or denying to shareholders the pre-emptive right to acquire additional or treasury shares of the corporation are: _____

_____

_____.

TENTH Provisions for regulating the internal affairs of the corporation are: _____

_____

_____.

ELEVENTH The address of the initial registered office of the corporation is: _____

_____

_____

and the name of its initial registered agent upon whom process may be served at such address is:

_____.

TWELFTH The number of directors constituting the initial board of directors of the corporation is _____, and the names and addresses of the persons who are to serve as directors until the first annual meeting of shareholders or until their successors are elected and shall qualify are:

_____   _____
Name   Name

_____   _____
Address   Address

_____   _____
Name   Name

_____   _____
Address   Address

THIRTEENTH The signatures, names and addresses of each incorporator are:

_____   _____
Signature   Signature

_____   _____
Print Name   Print Name

_____   _____
Address   Address

_____   _____
Signature   Signature

_____   _____
Print Name   Print Name

_____   _____
Address   Address

STATE OF NEW YORK
COUNTY OF
On _____ before me _____,
appeared _____ incorporator, _____
incorporator, _____ incorporator, _____
incorporator, personally known to me (or proved to me on the basis of satisfactory evidence) to be the person(s) whose name(s) is/are subscribed to the within instrument and acknowledged to me that he/she/they executed the same in his/her/their authorized capacity(ies), and that by his/her/their signature(s) on the instrument the person(s), or the entity on behalf of which the person(s) acted, executed this instrument. WITNESS my hand and official seal.

_____
Notary Public

(Seal)

Affiant _____Known_____Produced ID
Type if ID _____

140

Glossary of useful terms

A-C

Assets

Anything owned with monetary value. This includes both real and personal property.

Authorized shares

The number of shares a corporation is authorized to sell.

Bylaws

Rules adopted by the corporation itself for the regulation of a corporation's own actions; a subordinate law adopted by a corporation, association, or other body for its self-government or to regulate the rights and duties of its officers and members.

C corporation

A regular corporation that is not an S corporation.

Calendar year

The accounting year beginning on January 1 and ending on December 31.

Certificate or Articles of Incorporation

The document that creates a corporation according to the laws of the state. This must be filed and approved by the state.

C-I

Consolidation

When two corporations combine, creating a third.

Deceptively similar

A name so similar to another name that the two become confused in the public eye.

Dividend income

Dividends that must be declared as regular income for income tax purposes.

Fiscal year

Any 12-month period used by a business as its fiscal accounting period. Such accounting period may, for example, run from July 1 of one year through June 30 of the next year.

Foreign corporation

A corporation formed in one state or country but conducting some or all of its business in another state or country.

Incorporate

To form a corporation or to organize and be granted status as a corporation by following procedures prescribed by law.

Incorporator

The person who signs the Articles of Incorporation upon petitioning the state for a corporate charter.

Insolvency

Being able to pay one's debts; bankruptcy

Issued shares

The number of shares actually sold by the corporation.

M-P

Merger

The absorption of one corporation by another.

Minority stockholder

One who owns or controls less than 50 percent of the stock in a corporation.

Minutes

Written records of formal proceedings of stockholders' and directors' meetings.

Non-par value stock

Shares of stock without specified value.

Not-for-profit corporation

A corporation organized for some charitable, civil, social or other purpose that does not entail the generation of profit or the distribution of its income to members, principals, shareholders, officers or others affiliated with it. Such corporations are accorded special treatment under the law for some purposes, including taxation.

Parliamentary procedure

Rules such as "Roberts Rules of Order," which govern stockholders' meetings, directors' meetings, etc.

Par value stock

Shares of stock with a specified value.

Proxy

Authorization by a stockholder allowing another to vote his shares of stock.

P-S

Publicly owned corporation

One whose stock is owned by more than 25 stockholders and is regulated by the Securities and Exchange Commission.

Quorum

A majority of the stockholders or directors necessary for vote-counting and decision-making at a meeting. While a quorum is usually a majority of either the total membership or the members present, a quorum may consist of a greater number than a simple majority if desired and stated in the bylaws.

Regular corporation

Also known as a C Corporation.

Service business

A business that sells service or advice instead of a tangible product.

Shareholder

See Stockholder.

Start-up venture

A new business having no track record.

State statutes

Laws created by a state legislature.

Statutory agent

A lawyer, corporation or individual who has assumed the responsibility of being the legal representative for the corporation for purposes of accepting legal service in a certain state.

S-Su

S Corporation (Subchapter S Corporation)

A small business corporation which elects to be taxed as a partnership or proprietorship for federal income tax purposes. Individual shareholders enjoy the benefits under state law of limited corporate liability, but avoid corporate federal taxes.

Stock certificate

Written instrument evidencing a share in the ownership of a corporation.

Stockholder

A holder of one or more shares of the stock of a corporation. A stockholder may be called a "shareholder."

Subsidiary

A corporation owned by another corporation.

Resources

••• Departments of Incorporation •••

ALABAMA
Secretary of State
State Capitol Corporations Div.
P.O. Box 5616
Montgomery, AL 36103-5616
(334) 242-5324

ALASKA
State of Alaska
Department of Commerce and
Economic Development
Div. of Banking, Securities &
Corporations
Juneau, AL 99811-0807
(907) 465-2521

ARIZONA
Arizona Corporation Commission
Incorporating Division
1300 W. Washington St., 3rd Floor
Phoenix, AZ 85007
(602) 542-4786

ARKANSAS
Secretary of State–Corporations Div.
Aegon Building
501 Woodlane, Suite 310
Little Rock, AR 72201-1094
(501) 682-3409

CALIFORNIA
Secretary of State
1500 11th Street, 6th Floor
Sacramento, CA 95814
(916) 657-5448

COLORADO
Secretary of State
1560 Broadway, Suite 200
Denver, CO 80202
(303) 894-2200

CONNECTICUT
Office of the Secretary of State
State of Connecticut
Corporations Division
30 Trinity Street
Hartford, CT 06106
(860) 509-6000

DELAWARE
State of Delaware
Division of Corporations
P.O. Box 898
Dover, DE 19903
(302) 739-3073

DISTRICT OF COLUMBIA
Dept. of Consumer Reg. Affairs
614 "H" Street N.W., Rm 407
Washington, DC 20001
(202) 727-7278

FLORIDA
Division of Corporations
P.O. Box 6327
Tallahassee, FL 32314
(850) 488-9000

GEORGIA
Secretary of State
Corporations Department
2 Martin Luther King Junior Drive
Suite 315, West Tower
Atlanta, GA 30334
(404) 656-2817

HAWAII
Dept. of Commerce & Consumer Affairs
Business Registration Division
P.O. Box 40
Honolulu, HI 96810
(808) 586-2744

IDAHO
Secretary of State
P.O. Box 83720
Boise, ID 83720-0080
(208) 334-2300

ILLINOIS
Secretary of State
Department of Corporations
328 Howlett Building-Business Services
Springfield, IL 62756
(217) 782-7880

INDIANA
Secretary of State-Corporation Division
302 W. Washington St., Rm E018
Indianapolis, IN 46204
(317) 232-6576

IOWA
Secretary of State-Corporation Division
Hoover Blvd. 2nd Floor
Des Moines, IA 50319
(515) 281-7563

KANSAS
Secretary of State
Statehouse, 2nd Floor
300 SW 10th Street
Topeka, KS 66612-1594
(913) 296-4564

KENTUCKY
Secretary of State–Corporations Div.
152 Capitol Building
700 Capitol Avenue
Frankfort, KY 40601
(502) 564-2848

LOUISIANA
Secretary of State–Corporations Div.
P.O. Box 94125
Baton Rouge, LA 70804-9125
(504) 925-4716

MAINE
Secretary of State
Department of Incorporation
101 State House Station
Augusta, ME 04333-0101
(207) 287-6308

MARYLAND
State Dept. of Assess. and Tax.
301 W. Preston St., Room 809
Baltimore, MD 21201-2395
(410) 767-1340

MASSACHUSETTS
Secretary of State
Corporations Division
State House Room 337
Boston, MA 02133
(617) 727-2853

MICHIGAN
State of Michigan
Dept of Commerce, Corp. Div.
6546 Mercantile Way
Lansing, MI 48911
(517) 334-7561

MINNESOTA
Secretary of State
100 Constitution Avenue, Rm 180
St. Paul, MN 55155-1299
(612) 215-1441

MISSISSIPPI
Secretary of State
Office of Incorporation
P.O. Box 136
Jackson, MS 39205
(601) 359-1350

MISSOURI
Secretary of State–Corporations Div.
P.O. Box 778
Jefferson City, MO 65102
(573) 751-1301

MONTANA
Secretary of State
P.O. Box 202801
Helena, MT 59620-2801
(406) 444-2034

NEBRASKA
Secretary of State
Corporate Division
P.O. Box 94608
Lincoln, NB 68509
(402) 471-4079

NEVADA
Secretary of State
101 N. Carson Street
Carson City, NV 89701
(702) 687-5203

NEW HAMPSHIRE
Secretary of State–Corporations Div.
State House
107 Main Street, Room 204
Concord, NH 03301-4989
(603) 271-3246

NEW JERSEY
Secretary of State
P.O. Box 300
Trenton, NJ 08625
(609) 530-6431

NEW MEXICO
State Corporation Commission
P.O. Box 1269
Santa Fe, NM 87504-1269
(505) 827-4500

NEW YORK
Secretary of State–Corporations Div.
41 State Street
Albany, NY 12231
(518) 474-6200

NORTH CAROLINA
Secretary of State–Corporations Div.
300 North Salisbury Street
Raleigh, NC 27603-5909
(919) 733-4161

NORTH DAKOTA
Secretary of State–Corporations Div.
600 East Boulevard Avenue
Bismark, ND 58505
(701) 328-4284

OHIO
Secretary of State
30 East Broad Street, 14th Floor
Columbus, OH 43266-0418
(614) 466-1145

OKLAHOMA
Secretary of State
2300 N. Lincoln, Room 101
Oklahoma City, OK 73105
(405) 521-3911

OREGON
Secretary of State
Corporation Division
255 Capitol Street NE
Salem, OR 97310-1327
(503) 986-2200

PENNSYLVANIA
Commonwealth of Pennsylvania
Corporations Office
North Office Bldg., Room 302
Harrisburg, PA 17120
(717) 787-4057

PUERTO RICO
Commonwealth of Puerto Rico
Department of State
PO Box 9023271
San Juan, PR 00902-3271
(787) 722-2121

RHODE ISLAND
Secretary of State
Corporations Office
State House, Room 220
Providence, RI 02903
(401) 277-3040

SOUTH CAROLINA
Secretary of State
P.O. Box 11350
Columbia, SC 29211
(803) 734-2158

SOUTH DAKOTA
Secretary of State
Attn: Corporations
500 E. Capitol, Suite 204
Pierre, SD 57501
(605) 773-4845

TENNESSEE
Secretary of State–Corporations Div.
State Capitol, 1st Floor
Nashville, TN 37243-0305
(615) 741-0529

TEXAS
Secretary of State–Corporations Div.
P.O. Box 13697
Austin, TX 78711-3697
(512) 463-5586

UTAH
Department of Commerce
P.O. Box 146791
Salt Lake City, UT 84114-6701
(801) 530-6027

VERMONT
Secretary of State
Corporations Division
109 State Street
Montpelier, VT 05609-1101
(802) 828-2386

VIRGINIA
Commonwealth of Virginia
State Corporation Commission
P.O. Box 1197
Richmond, VA 23218
(804) 371-9376

WASHINGTON
Secretary of State
Corporation Division
P.O. Box 40220
Olympia, WA 98504-0220
(360) 753-2896

WEST VIRGINIA
Secretary of State–Corporations Div.
1900 Kanawha Boulevard E
Building 1, Suite 157-K
Charleston, WV 25305-0770
(304) 558-8000

WISCONSIN
Department of Financial Institutions
Corporations and Consumer Division
P.O. Box 7846
Madison, WI 53707-7846
(608) 261-7577

WYOMING
Secretary of State
Corporations Division
State Capitol Bldg.
Cheyenne, WY 82002-0020
(307) 777-7314

••• Online Resources •••

◆ **American Arbitration Association**

URL: *http://www.adr.org*

◆ **American Consumer Credit Counseling**

URL: *http://www.consumercredit.com*

◆ **American Express Small Business Exchange**

URL: *http://www.americanexpress.com/smallbusiness*

◆ **American Society of Corporate Secretaries**

URL: *http://www.ascs.org*

◆ **BizProWeb**

URL: *http://www.bizproweb.com*

◆ **Commercial Law League of America**

URL: *http://www.clla.org*

◆ **Corporate Finance Network–Corporate Governance**

URL: *http://www.corpfinet.com/EP_Corp_Gov.html*

◆ **Council of Better Business Bureaus, Inc.**

URL: *http://www.bbb.org*

◆ **Education Index, Business Resources**

URL: *http://www.educationindex.com/bus*

◆ **Employmentlawcenteral**

URL: *http://www.employmentlawcenteral.com*

◆ **Entrepreneur's Help Page**

URL: *http://www.tannedfeet.com*

◆ **Federal Trade Commission-Consumer Protection**

URL: *http://www.ftc.gov/bcp/menu-credit.htm*

◆ **Garrett Publishing, Inc.**

URL: *http://www.garrettpub.com*

◆ **International Finance & Commodities Institute**

URL: *http://finance.wat.ch/IFCI*

◆ **Lawlounge**

URL: *http://lawlounge.com/topics/corporate/main.htm*

◆ **National Association of Corporate Directors**

URL: *http://www.nacdonline.org/seminar_entrepren.htm*

◆ **National Center for Employee Ownership**

URL: *http://www.nceo.org/index.html*

◆ **National Employee Rights Institute, NERI**

URL: *http://www.nerinet.org*

◆ **National Federation of Independent Business**

URL: *http://www.nfibonline.com*

◆ **National Small Business Development Center Research Network**

URL: *http://www.smallbiz.suny.edu*

◆ **Small Business Advisor**

URL: *http://www.isquare.com*

◆ **Small Business Primer**

URL: *http://www.ces.ncsu.edu/depts/fcs/business/*
welcome.html

◆ **U.S. Department of Labor**

URL: *http://dol.gov/dol/welcome.htm*

◆ **U.S. Small Business Administration**

URL: *http://www.sbaonline.sba.gov/starting*

••• Legal Search Engines •••

◆ **All Law**

 URL: *http://www.alllaw.com*

◆ **American Law Sources On Line**

 URL: *http://www.lawsource.com/also/searchfm.htm*

◆ **Catalaw**

 URL: *http://www.catalaw.com*

◆ **FindLaw**

 URL: *http://www.findlaw.com*

◆ **Hieros Gamos**

 URL: *http://www.hg.org/hg.html*

◆ **InternetOracle**

 URL: *http://www.internetoracle.com/legal.htm*

◆ **LawAid**

 URL: *http://www.lawaid.com/search.html*

◆ **LawCrawler**

 URL: *http://www.lawcrawler.com*

◆ **LawEngine, The**

  URL: http://www.fastsearch.com/law

◆ **LawRunner**

  URL: http://www.lawrunner.com

◆ **'Lectric Law Library™**

  URL: http://www.lectlaw.com

◆ **Legal Search Engines**

  URL: http://www.dreamscape.com/frankvad/search.legal.html

◆ **LEXIS/NEXIS Communications Center**

  URL: http://www.lexis-nexis.com/lncc/general/search.html

◆ **Meta-Index for U.S. Legal Research**

  URL: http://gsulaw.gsu.edu/metaindex

◆ **Seamless Website, The**

  URL: http://seamless.com

◆ **USALaw**

  URL: http://www.usalaw.com/linksrch.cfm

◆ **WestLaw**

  URL: http://westlaw.com (Registered users only. Fee paid service.)

••• State Bar Associations •••

ALABAMA

Alabama State Bar
415 Dexter Avenue
Montgomery, AL 36104

mailing address:
PO Box 671
Montgomery, AL 36101
(334) 269-1515

http://www.alabar.org

ALASKA

Alaska Bar Association
510 L Street No. 602
Anchorage, AK 99501

mailing address
PO Box 100279
Anchorage, AK 99510

ARIZONA

State Bar of Arizona
111 West Monroe
Phoenix, AZ 85003-1742
(602) 252-4804

ARKANSAS

Arkansas Bar Association
400 West Markham
Little Rock, AR 72201
(501) 375-4605

CALIFORNIA

State Bar of California
555 Franklin Street
San Francisco, CA 94102
(415) 561-8200

http://www.calbar.org

Alameda County Bar
Association

http://www.acbanet.org

COLORADO

Colorado Bar Association
No. 950, 1900 Grant Street
Denver, CO 80203
(303) 860-1115

http://www.cobar.org

CONNECTICUT

Connecticut Bar Association
101 Corporate Place
Rocky Hill, CT 06067-1894
(203) 721-0025

DELAWARE

Delaware State Bar Association
1225 King Street, 10th floor
Wilmington, DE 19801
(302) 658-5279
(302) 658-5278 (lawyer referral service)

DISTRICT OF COLUMBIA

District of Columbia Bar
1250 H Street, NW, 6th Floor
Washington, DC 20005
(202) 737-4700

Bar Association of the District of
Columbia
1819 H Street, NW, 12th floor
Washington, DC 20006-3690
(202) 223-6600

FLORIDA

The Florida Bar
The Florida Bar Center
650 Apalachee Parkway
Tallahassee, FL 32399-2300
(850) 561-5600

GEORGIA

State Bar of Georgia
800 The Hurt Building
50 Hurt Plaza
Atlanta, GA 30303
(404) 527-8700

http://www.gabar.com

HAWAII

Hawaii State Bar Association
1136 Union Mall
Penthouse 1
Honolulu, HI 96813
(808) 537-1868

http://www.hsba.org

IDAHO

Idaho State Bar
PO Box 895
Boise, ID 83701
(208) 334-4500

ILLINOIS

Illinois State Bar Association
424 South Second Street
Springfield, IL 62701
(217) 525-1760

INDIANA

Indiana State Bar Association
230 East Ohio Street
Indianapolis, IN 46204
(317) 639-5465

http://www.iquest.net/isba

IOWA

Iowa State Bar Association
521 East Locust
Des Moines, IA 50309
(515) 243-3179

http://www.iowabar.org

KANSAS

Kansas Bar Association
1200 Harrison Street
Topeka, KS 66601
(913) 234-5696

http://www.ink.org/public/
                              cybar

KENTUCKY

Kentucky Bar Association
514 West Main Street
Frankfort, KY 40601-1883
(502) 564-3795

http://www.kybar.org

LOUISIANA

Louisiana State Bar Association
601 St. Charles Avenue
New Orleans, LA 70130
(504) 566-1600

MAINE

Maine State Bar Association
124 State Street
PO Box 788
Augusta, ME 04330
(207) 622-7523

http://www.mainebar.org

MARYLAND

Maryland State Bar Association
520 West Fayette Street
Baltimore, MD 21201
(301) 685-7878

http://www.msba.org/msba

MASSACHUSETTS

Massachusetts Bar Association
20 West Street
Boston, MA 02111
(617) 542-3602
(617) 542-9103 (lawyer referral service)

MICHIGAN

State Bar of Michigan
306 Townsend Street
Lansing, MI 48933-2083
(517) 372-9030

http://www.michbar.org

MINNESOTA

Minnesota State Bar Association
514 Nicollet Mall
Minneapolis, MN 55402
(612) 333-1183

MISSISSIPPI

The Mississippi Bar
643 No. State Street
Jackson, Mississippi 39202
(601) 948-4471

MISSOURI

The Missouri Bar
P.O. Box 119, 326 Monroe
Jefferson City, Missouri 65102
(314) 635-4128

http://www.mobar.org

MONTANA

State Bar of Montana
46 North Main
PO Box 577
Helena, MT 59624
(406) 442-7660

NEBRASKA

Nebraska State Bar Association
635 South 14th Street, 2nd floor
Lincoln, NE 68508
(402) 475-7091

http://www.nebar.com

NEVADA

State Bar of Nevada
201 Las Vegas Blvd.
Las Vegas, NV 89101
(702) 382-2200

http://www.nvbar.org

NEW HAMPSHIRE

New Hampshire Bar Association
112 Pleasant Street
Concord, NH 03301
(603) 224-6942

NEW JERSEY

New Jersey State Bar Association
One Constitution Square
New Brunswuck, NJ 08901-1500
(908) 249-5000

NEW MEXICO

State Bar of New Mexico
121 Tijeras Street N.E.
Albuquerque, NM 87102

mailing address:
PO Box 25883
Albuquerque, NM 87125
(505) 843-6132

NEW YORK

New York State Bar Association
One Elk Street
Albany, NY 12207
(518) 463-3200

http://www.nysba.org

NORTH CAROLINA

North Carolina State Bar
208 Fayetteville Street Mall
Raleigh, NC 27601

mailing address:
PO Box 25908
Raleigh, NC 27611
(919) 828-4620

North Carolina Bar Association
1312 Annapolis Drive
Raleigh, NC 27608

mailing address:
PO Box 12806
Raleigh, NC 27605
(919) 828-0561

http://www.barlinc.org

NORTH DAKOTA

State Bar Association of North
Dakota
515 1/2 East Broadway, suite 101
Bismarck, ND 58501

mailing address:
PO Box 2136
Bismarck, ND 58502
(701) 255-1404

OHIO

Ohio State Bar Association
1700 Lake Shore Drive
Columbus, OH 43204

mailing address:
PO Box 16562
Columbus, OH 43216-6562
(614) 487-2050

OKLAHOMA

Oklahoma Bar Association
1901 North Lincoln
Oklahoma City, OK 73105
(405) 524-2365

OREGON

Oregon State Bar
5200 S.W. Meadows Road
PO Box 1689
Lake Oswego, OR 97035-0889
(503) 620-0222

PENNSYLVANIA

Pennsylvannia Bar Association
100 South Street
PO Box 186
Harrisburg, PA 17108
(717) 238-6715

Pennsylvania Bar Institute
http://www.pbi.org

PUERTO RICO

Puerto Rico Bar Association
PO Box 1900
San Juan, Puerto Rico 00903
(787) 721-3358

RHODE ISLAND

Rhode Island Bar Association
115 Cedar Street
Providence, RI 02903
(401) 421-5740

SOUTH CAROLINA

South Carolina Bar
950 Taylor Street
PO Box 608
Columbia, SC 29202
(803) 799-6653

http://www.scbar.org

SOUTH DAKOTA

State Bar of South Dakota
222 East Capitol
Pierre, SD 57501
(605) 224-7554

TENNESSEE

Tennessee Bar Assn
3622 West End Avenue
Nashville, TN 37205
(615) 383-7421

http://www.tba.org

TEXAS

State Bar of Texas
1414 Colorado
PO Box 12487
Austin, TX 78711
(512) 463-1463

UTAH

Utah State Bar
645 South 200 East, Suite 310
Salt Lake City, UT 84111
(801) 531-9077

VERMONT

Vermont Bar Association
PO Box 100
Montpelier, VT 05601
(802) 223-2020

VIRGINIA

Virginia State Bar
707 East Main Street, suite 1500
Richmond, VA 23219-0501
(804) 775-0500

Virginia Bar Association
701 East Franklin St., Suite 1120
Richmond, VA 23219
(804) 644-0041

VIRGIN ISLANDS

Virgin Islands Bar Association
P.O. Box 4108
Christiansted, Virgin Islands
00822
(340) 778-7497

WASHINGTON

Washington State Bar
Association
500 Westin Street
2001 Sixth Avenue
Seattle, WA 98121-2599
(206) 727-8200

http://www.wsba.org

WEST VIRGINIA

West Virginia State Bar
2006 Kanawha Blvd. East
Charleston, WV 25311
(304) 558-2456

http://www.wvbar.org

West Virginia Bar Association
904 Security Building
100 Capitol Street
Charleston, WV 25301
(304) 342-1474

WISCONSIN

State Bar of Wisconsin
402 West Wilson Street
Madison, WI 53703
(608) 257-3838

http://www.wisbar.org/
                    home.htm

WYOMING

Wyoming State Bar
500 Randall Avenue
Cheyenne, WY 82001
PO Box 109
Cheyenne, WY 82003
(307) 632-9061

How to save on attorney fees

Triplex
Graphics,
Inc.

How to save on attorney fees

Triplex Graphics, Inc.

Millions of Americans know they need legal protection, whether it's to get agreements in writing, protect themselves from lawsuits, or document business transactions. But too often these basic but important legal matters are neglected because of something else millions of Americans know: legal services are expensive.

They don't have to be. In response to the demand for affordable legal protection and services, there are now specialized clinics that process simple documents. Paralegals help people prepare legal claims on a freelance basis. People find they can handle their own legal affairs with do-it-yourself legal guides and kits. Indeed, this book is a part of this growing trend.

When are these alternatives to a lawyer appropriate? If you hire an attorney, how can you make sure you're getting good advice for a reasonable fee? Most importantly, do you know how to lower your legal expenses?

When there is no alternative

Make no mistake: serious legal matters require a lawyer. The tips in this book can help you reduce your legal fees, but there is no alternative to good professional legal services in certain circumstances:

- when you are charged with a felony, you are a repeat offender, or jail is possible

- when a substantial amount of money or property is at stake in a lawsuit

- when you are a party in an adversarial divorce or custody case

- when you are an alien facing deportation

- when you are the plaintiff in a personal injury suit that involves large sums of money

- when you're involved in very important transactions

Are you sure you want to take it to court?

Consider the following questions before you pursue legal action:

What are your financial resources?

Money buys experienced attorneys, and experience wins over first-year lawyers and public defenders. Even with a strong case, you may save money by not going to court. Yes, people win millions in court. But for every big winner there are ten plaintiffs who either lose or win so little that litigation wasn't worth their effort.

Do you have the time and energy for a trial?

Courts are overbooked, and by the time your case is heard your initial zeal may have grown cold. If you can, make a reasonable settlement out of court. On personal matters, like a divorce or custody case, consider the emotional toll on all parties. Any legal case will affect you in some way. You will need time away from work. A newsworthy case may bring press coverage. Your loved ones, too, may face publicity. There is usually good reason to settle most cases quickly, quietly, and economically.

How can you settle disputes without litigation?

Consider *mediation*. In mediation, each party pays half the mediator's fee and, together, they attempt to work out a compromise informally. *Binding arbitration* is another alternative. For a small fee, a trained specialist serves as judge, hears both sides, and hands down a ruling that both parties have agreed to accept.

So you need an attorney

Having done your best to avoid litigation, if you still find yourself headed for court, you will need an attorney. To get the right attorney at a reasonable cost, be guided by these four questions:

What type of case is it?

You don't seek a foot doctor for a toothache. Find an attorney experienced in your type of legal problem. If you can get recommendations from clients who have recently won similar cases, do so.

Where will the trial be held?

You want a lawyer familiar with that court system and one who knows the court personnel and the local protocol—which can vary from one locality to another.

Should you hire a large or small firm?

Hiring a senior partner at a large and prestigious law firm sounds reassuring, but chances are the actual work will be handled by associates—at high rates. Small firms may give your case more attention but, with fewer resources, take longer to get the work done.

What can you afford?

Hire an attorney you can afford, of course, but know what a fee quote includes. High fees may reflect a firm's luxurious offices, high-paid staff and unmonitored expenses, while low estimates may mean "unexpected" costs later. Ask for a written estimate of all costs and anticipated expenses.

How to find a good lawyer

Whether you need an attorney quickly or you're simply open to future possibilities, here are seven nontraditional methods for finding your lawyer:

1) **Word of mouth**: Successful lawyers develop reputations. Your friends, business associates and other professionals are potential referral sources. But beware of hiring a friend. Keep the client-attorney relationship strictly business.

2) **Directories**: The Yellow Pages and the Martin-Hubbell Lawyer Directory (in your local library) can help you locate a lawyer with the right education, background and expertise for your case.

3) **Databases**: A paralegal should be able to run a quick computer search of local attorneys for you using the Westlaw or Lexis database.

4) **State bar associations**: Bar associations are listed in phone books. Along with lawyer referrals, your bar association can direct you to low-cost legal clinics or specialists in your area.

5) **Law schools**: Did you know that a legal clinic run by a law school gives law students hands-on experience? This may fit your legal needs. A third-year law student loaded with enthusiasm and a little experience might fill the bill quite inexpensively—or even for free.

6) **Advertisements**: Ads are a lawyer's business card. If a "TV attorney" seems to have a good track record with your kind of case, why not call? Just don't be swayed by the glamour of a high-profile attorney.

7) **Your own ad**: A small ad describing the qualifications and legal expertise you're seeking, placed in a local bar association journal, may get you just the lead you need.

How to hire and work with your attorney

No matter how you hear about an attorney, you must interview him or her in person. Call the office during business hours and ask to speak to the attorney directly. Then explain your case briefly and mention how you obtained the attorney's name. If the attorney sounds interested and knowledgeable, arrange for a visit.

The ten-point visit

1) Note the address. This is a good indication of the rates to expect.

2) Note the condition of the offices. File-laden desks and poorly maintained work space may indicate a poorly run firm.

3) Look for up-to-date computer equipment and an adequate complement of support personnel.

4) Note the appearance of the attorney. How will he or she impress a judge or jury?

5) Is the attorney attentive? Does the attorney take notes, ask questions, follow up on points you've mentioned?

6)   Ask what schools he or she has graduated from, and feel free to check credentials with the state bar association.

7)   Does the attorney have a good track record with your type of case?

8)   Does he or she explain legal terms to you in plain English?

9)   Are the firm's costs reasonable?

10)   Will the attorney provide references?

Hiring the attorney

Having chosen your attorney, make sure all the terms are agreeable. Send letters to any other attorneys you have interviewed, thanking them for their time and interest in your case and explaining that you have retained another attorney's services.

Request a letter from your new attorney outlining your retainer agreement. The letter should list all fees you will be responsible for as well as the billing arrangement. Did you arrange to pay in installments? This should be noted in your retainer agreement.

Controlling legal costs

Legal fees and expenses can get out of control easily, but the client who is willing to put in the effort can keep legal costs manageable. Work out a budget with your attorney. Create a timeline for your case. Estimate the costs involved in each step.

Legal fees can be straightforward. Some lawyers charge a fixed rate for a specific project. Others charge contingency fees (they collect a percentage of your recovery, usually 35-50 percent if you win and nothing if you lose). But most attorneys prefer to bill by the hour. Expenses can run the gamut, with one hourly charge for taking depositions and another for making copies.

Have your attorney give you a list of charges for services rendered and an itemized monthly bill. The bill should explain the service performed, who performed the work, when the service was provided, how long it took, and how the service benefits your case.

Ample opportunity abounds in legal billing for dishonesty and greed. There is also plenty of opportunity for knowledgeable clients to cut their bills significantly if they know what to look for. Asking the right questions and setting limits on fees is smart and can save you a bundle. Don't be afraid to question legal bills. It's your case and your money!

When the bill arrives

- **Retainer fees**: You should already have a written retainer agreement. Ideally, the retainer fee applies toward case costs, and your agreement puts that in writing. Protect yourself by escrowing the retainer fee until the case has been handled to your satisfaction.

- **Office visit charges**: Track your case and all documents, correspondence, and bills. Diary all dates, deadlines and questions you want to ask your attorney during your next office visit. This keeps expensive office visits focused and productive, with more accomplished in less time. If your attorney charges less for phone consultations than office visits, reserve visits for those tasks that must be done in person.

- **Phone bills**: This is where itemized bills are essential. Who made the call, who was spoken to, what was discussed, when was the call made, and how long did it last? Question any charges that seem unnecessary or excessive (over 60 minutes).

- **Administrative costs**: Your case may involve hundreds, if not thousands, of documents: motions, affidavits, depositions, interrogatories, bills, memoranda, and letters. Are they all necessary? Understand your attorney's case strategy before paying for an endless stream of costly documents.

- **Associate and paralegal fees**: Note in your retainer agreement which staff people will have access to your file. Then you'll have an informed and efficient staff working on your case, and you'll recognize their names on your bill. Of course, your attorney should handle the important part of your case, but less costly paralegals or associates may handle routine matters more economically. Note: Some firms expect their associates to meet a quota of billable hours, although the time spent is not always warranted. Review your bill. Does the time spent make sense for the document in question? Are several staff involved in matters that should be handled by one person? Don't be afraid to ask questions. And withhold payment until you have satisfactory answers.

- **Court stenographer fees**: Depositions and court hearings require costly transcripts and stenographers. This means added expenses. Keep an eye on these costs.

- **Copying charges**: Your retainer fee should limit the number of copies made of your complete file. This is in your legal interest, because multiple files mean multiple chances others may access your confidential information. It is also in your financial interest, because copying costs can be astronomical.

- **Fax costs**: As with the phone and copier, the fax can easily run up costs. Set a limit.

- **Postage charges**: Be aware of how much it costs to send a legal document overnight, or a registered letter. Offer to pick up or deliver expensive items when it makes sense.

- **Filing fees**: Make it clear to your attorney that you want to minimize the number of court filings in your case. Watch your bill and question any filing that seems unnecessary.

- **Document production fee**: Turning over documents to your opponent is mandatory and expensive. If you're faced with reproducing boxes of documents, consider having the job done by a commercial firm rather than your attorney's office.

- **Research and investigations**: Pay only for photographs that can be used in court. Can you hire a photographer at a lower rate than what your attorney charges? Reserve that right in your retainer agreement. Database research can also be extensive and expensive; if your attorney uses Westlaw or Nexis, set limits on the research you will pay for.

- **Expert witnesses**: Question your attorney if you are expected to pay for more than a reasonable number of expert witnesses. Limit the number to what is essential to your case.

- **Technology costs**: Avoid videos, tape recordings, and graphics if you can use old-fashioned diagrams to illustrate your case.

- **Travel expenses**: Travel expenses for those connected to your case can be quite costly unless you set a maximum budget. Check all travel-related items on your bill, and make sure they are appropriate. Always question why the travel is necessary before you agree to pay for it.

- **Appeals costs**: Losing a case often means an appeal, but weigh the costs involved before you make that decision. If money is at stake, do a cost-benefit analysis to see if an appeal is financially justified.

- **Monetary damages**: Your attorney should be able to help you estimate the total damages you will have to pay if you lose a civil case. Always consider settling out of court rather than proceeding to trial when the trial costs will be high.

- **Surprise costs**: Surprise costs are so routine they're predictable. The judge may impose unexpected court orders on one or both sides, or the opposition will file an unexpected motion that increases your legal costs. Budget a few thousand dollars over what you estimate your case will cost. It usually is needed.

- **Padded expenses**: Assume your costs and expenses are legitimate. But some firms do inflate expenses—office supplies, database searches, copying, postage, phone bills—to bolster their bottom line. Request copies of bills your law firm receives from support services. If you are not the only client represented on a bill, determine those charges related to your case.

Keeping it legal without a lawyer

The best way to save legal costs is to avoid legal problems. There are hundreds of ways to decrease your chances of lawsuits and other nasty legal encounters. Most simply involve a little common sense. You can also use your own initiative to find and use the variety of self-help legal aid available to consumers.

11 situations in which you may not need a lawyer

1) **No-fault divorce**: Married couples with no children, minimal property, and no demands for alimony can take advantage of divorce mediation services. A lawyer should review your divorce agreement before you sign it, but you will have saved a fortune in attorney fees. A marital or family counselor may save a seemingly doomed marriage, or help both parties move beyond anger to a calm settlement. Either way, counseling can save you money.

2) **Wills**: Do-it-yourself wills and living trusts are ideal for people with estates of less than $600,000. Even if an attorney reviews your final documents, a will kit allows you to read the documents, ponder your bequests, fill out sample forms, and discuss your wishes with your family at your leisure, without a lawyer's meter running.

3) **Incorporating**: Incorporating a small business can be done by any business owner. Your state government office provides the forms and instructions necessary. A visit to your state office will probably be

necessary to perform a business name check. A fee of $100-$200 is usually charged for processing your Articles of Incorporation. The rest is paperwork: filling out forms correctly; holding regular, official meetings; and maintaining accurate records.

4) **Routine business transactions**: Copyrights, for example, can be applied for by asking the U.S. Copyright Office for the appropriate forms and brochures. The same is true of the U.S. Patent and Trademark Office. If your business does a great deal of document preparation and research, hire a certified paralegal rather than paying an attorney's rates. Consider mediation or binding arbitration rather than going to court for a business dispute. Hire a human resources/benefits administrator to head off disputes concerning discrimination or other employee charges.

5) **Repairing bad credit**: When money matters get out of hand, attorneys and bankruptcy should not be your first solution. Contact a credit counseling organization that will help you work out manageable payment plans so that everyone wins. It can also help you learn to manage your money better. A good company to start with is the Consumer Credit Counseling Service, 1-800-388-2227.

6) **Small Claims Court**: For legal grievances amounting to a few thousand dollars in damages, represent yourself in Small Claims Court. There is a small filing fee, forms to fill out, and several court visits necessary. If you can collect evidence, state your case in a clear and logical presentation, and come across as neat, respectful and sincere, you can succeed in Small Claims Court.

7) **Traffic Court**: Like Small Claims Court, Traffic Court may show more compassion to a defendant appearing without an attorney. If you are ticketed for a minor offense and want to take it to court, you will be asked to plead guilty or not guilty. If you plead guilty, you can ask for leniency in sentencing by presenting mitigating circumstances. Bring any witnesses who can support your story, and remember that presentation (some would call it acting ability) is as important as fact.

8) **Residential zoning petition**: If a homeowner wants to open a home business, build an addition, or make other changes that may affect his or her neighborhood, town approval is required. But you don't need a lawyer to fill out a zoning variance application, turn it in, and present your story at a public hearing. Getting local support before the hearing is the best way to assure a positive vote; contact as many neighbors as possible to reassure them that your plans won't adversely affect them or the neighborhood.

9) **Government benefit applications**: Applying for veterans' or unemployment benefits may be daunting, but the process doesn't require legal help. Apply for either immediately upon becoming eligible. Note: If your former employer contests your application for unemployment benefits and you have to defend yourself at a hearing, you may want to consider hiring an attorney.

10) **Receiving government files**: The Freedom of Information Act gives every American the right to receive copies of government information about him or her. Write a letter to the appropriate state or federal agency, noting the precise information you want. List each document in a separate paragraph. Mention the Freedom of Information Act, and state that you will pay any expenses. Close with your signature and the address the documents should be sent to. An approved request may take six months to arrive. If it is refused on the grounds that the information is classified or violates another's privacy, send a letter of appeal explaining why the released information would not endanger anyone. Enlist the support of your local state or federal representative, if possible, to smooth the approval process.

11) **Citizenship**: Arriving in the United States to work and become a citizen is a process tangled in bureaucratic red tape, but it requires more perseverance than legal assistance. Immigrants can learn how to obtain a "Green Card," under what circumstances they can work, and what the requirements of citizenship are by contacting the Immigration Services or reading a good self-help book.

Save more; it's E-Z

When it comes to saving attorneys' fees, Made E-Z Products™ is the consumer's best friend. America's largest publisher of self-help legal products offers legally valid forms for virtually every situation. Made E-Z Kits and Made E-Z Guides include all necessary forms with a simple-to-follow manual of instructions or a layman's book. Made E-Z Books are a legal library of forms and documents for everyday business and personal needs. Made E-Z Software provides those same forms on disk and CD for customized documents at the touch of the keyboard.

You can add to your legal savvy and your ability to protect yourself, your loved ones, your business and your property with a range of self-help legal titles available through Made E-Z Products™. See the product descriptions and information at the back of this guide.

Save On Legal Fees

with software and books from Made E-Z Products™ available at your nearest bookstore, or call 1-800-822-4566

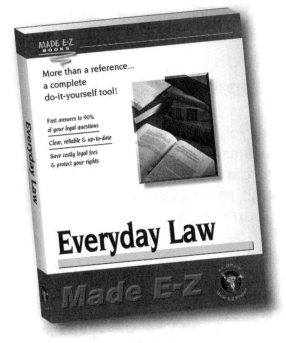

Stock No.: BK411
$24.95 8.5" x 11"
500 pages Soft cover

... Also available as
software—Stock No. SW1185

Everyday Law Made E-Z

The book that saves legal fees every time it's opened.

Here, in *Everyday Law Made E-Z*, are fast answers to 90% of the legal questions anyone is ever likely to ask, such as:

- How can I control my neighbor's pet?
- Can I change my name?
- What is a common law marriage?
- When should I incorporate my business?
- Is a child responsible for his bills?
- Who owns a husband's gifts to his wife?
- How do I become a naturalized citizen?
- Should I get my divorce in Nevada?
- Can I write my own will?
- Who is responsible when my son drives my car?
- How can my uncle get a Green Card?
- What are the rights of a non-smoker?
- Do I have to let the police search my car?
- What is sexual harassment?
- When is euthanasia legal?
- What repairs must my landlord make?
- What's the difference between fair criticism and slander?
- When can I get my deposit back?
- Can I sue the federal government?
- Am I responsible for a drunken guest's auto accident?
- Is a hotel liable if it does not honor a reservation?
- Does my car fit the lemon law?

Whether for personal or business use, this 500-page information-packed book helps the layman safeguard his property, avoid disputes, comply with legal obligations, and enforce his rights. Hundreds of cases illustrate thousands of points of law, each clearly and completely explained.

Whatever you need to know, we've made it E-Z!

Informative text and forms you can fill out on-screen.* From personal to business, legal to leisure—we've made it E-Z!

Personal & Family

For all your family's needs, we have titles that will help keep you organized and guide you through most every aspect of your personal life.

Business

Whether you're starting from scratch with a home business or you just want to keep your corporate records in shape, we've got the programs for you.

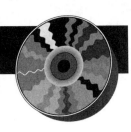

MADE E·Z® LIBRARY

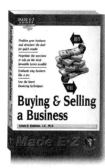

MADE E-Z GUIDES

Each comprehensive guide contains all the information you need to master one of dozens of topics, plus sample forms (if applicable).

Most guides also include an appendix of valuable resources, a handy glossary, and the valuable 14-page supplement "How to Save on Attorney Fees."

Advertising Your Business Made E-Z G327
Learn the secrets and use the tools of the professionals.

Asset Protection Made E-Z G320
Shelter your property from financial disaster.

Bankruptcy Made E-Z G300
Take the confusion out of filing bankruptcy.

Business Startups Made E-Z G344
Plan and start any home-based or small business.

Buying/Selling a Business Made E-Z G321
Position your business and structure the deal for quick results.

Buying/Selling Your Home Made E-Z G311
Buy or sell your home for the right price—right now.

Collecting Child Support Made E-Z G315
Enforce your rights as a single parent.

Credit Repair Made E-Z G303
All the tools to put you back on track.

Divorce Made E-Z G302
Proceed on your own, without a lawyer.

Employment Law Made E-Z G312
A handy reference for employers and employees.

Financing Your Business Made E-Z G322
Negotiate the best financing and grow your business.

Free Legal Help Made E-Z G339
Enforce your rights—without an expensive lawyer.

Free Stuff For Everyone Made E-Z G347
A complete roadmap to fabulous freebies.

Fund Raising Made E-Z G332
Magnetize big donations with simple ideas.

Get Out of Debt Made E-Z
Learn how to become debt-free.

Incorporation Made E-Z G301
Information you need to incorporate your company.

Last Will & Testament Made E-Z G307
Write a will the right way—the E-Z way.

Limited Liability Companies Made E-Z G316
Learn all about the hottest new business entity.

Living Trust Made E-Z G305
Trust us to help you provide for your loved ones.

Living Will Made E-Z G306
Take steps now to insure Death With Dignity.

Marketing Your Small Business Made E-Z G335
Proven marketing strategies for business success.

Money For College Made E-Z G334
Finance your college education—without the debt!

Multi-level Marketing Made E-Z G338
Turn your own product or service into an MLM empire.

Mutual Fund Investing Made E-Z G343
Build a secure future with fast-growth mutual funds.

Offshore Investing Made E-Z G337
Transfer your wealth offshore for financial privacy.

Owning a No-Cash-Down Business Made E-Z G336
Financial independence without risk, cash, or experience.

Partnerships Made E-Z G318
Avoid double taxation.

Profitable Mail Order Made E-Z G323
Turn virtually any product into a profitable mail order item.

SBA Loans Made E-Z G325
In-depth explanation of required and optional forms.

Selling On The Web Made E-Z G324
Wealth-building, web-building strategies for any size business.

Shoestring Investing Made E-Z G330
Amass more wealth with investments through strategic investing.

Stock Market Investing Made E-Z G331
Pick the best stocks and manage your own portfolio.

Solving Business Problems Made E-Z G326
Identify and solve business problems with proven strategies.

Solving IRS Problems Made E-Z G319
Settle with the IRS for pennies on the dollar.

Successful Resumes Made E-Z G346
Exploit your strengths, gain confidence, and secure that dream job

Winning Business Plans Made E-Z G342
Attract more capital—faster.

FEDERAL & STATE
Labor Law Posters

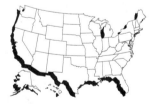

Made E-Z Software	ITEM #	QTY.	PRICE‡	EXTENSION
E-Z Construction Estimator	SS4300		$24.95	
E-Z Contractors' Forms	SS4301		$24.95	
Contractors' Business Builder Software Bundle	SS4002		$49.95	
Corporate Secretary	SS4003		$24.95	
Asset Protection Made E-Z	SS4304		$24.95	
Corporate Records Made E-Z	SS4305		$24.95	
Vital Records Made E-Z	SS4306		$24.95	
Managing Employees	SS4307		$24.95	
Accounting Made E-Z	SS4308		$24.95	
Limited Liability Companies (LLC)	SS4309		$24.95	
Partnerships	SS4310		$24.95	
Solving IRS Problems	SS4311		$24.95	
Winning In Small Claims Court	SS4312		$24.95	
Collecting Unpaid Bills Made E-Z	SS4313		$24.95	
Selling On The Web (E-Commerce)	SS4314		$24.95	
Your Profitable Home Business Made E-Z	SS4315		$24.95	
Get Out Of Debt Made E-Z	SS4317		$24.95	
E-Z Business Lawyer Library	SS4318		$49.95	
E-Z Estate Planner	SS4319		$49.95	
E-Z Personal Lawyer Library	SS4320		$49.95	
Payroll Made E-Z	SS4321		$24.95	
Personal Legal Forms and Agreements	SS4322		$24.95	
Business Legal Forms and Agreements	SS4323		$24.95	
Employee Policies and Manuals	SS4324		$24.95	
Incorporation Made E-Z	SW1176		$24.95	
Last Wills Made E-Z	SW1177		$24.95	
Everyday Law Made E-Z	SW1185		$24.95	
Everyday Legal Forms & Agreements Made E-Z	SW1186		$24.95	
Business Startups Made E-Z	SW1192		$24.95	
Credit Repair Made E-Z	SW2211		$24.95	
Business Forms Made E-Z	SW2223		$24.95	
Buying and Selling A Business Made E-Z	SW2242		$24.95	
Marketing Your Small Business Made E-Z	SW2245		$24.95	
Get Out Of Debt Made E-Z	SW2246		$24.95	
Winning Business Plans Made E-Z	SW2247		$24.95	
Successful Resumes Made E-Z	SW2248		$24.95	
Solving Business Problems Made E-Z	SW2249		$24.95	
Profitable Mail Order Made E-Z	SW2250		$24.95	
Deluxe Business Forms	SW2251		$49.95	
E-Z Small Business Library	SW2252		$49.95	
Sub-total for Software			$	
Made E-Z Guides				
Bankruptcy Made E-Z	G300		$14.95	
Incorporation Made E-Z	G301		$14.95	
Divorce Made E-Z	G302		$14.95	
Credit Repair Made E-Z	G303		$14.95	
Living Trusts Made E-Z	G305		$14.95	
Living Wills Made E-Z	G306		$14.95	
Last Will & Testament Made E-Z	G307		$14.95	
Buying/Selling Your Home Made E-Z	G311		$14.95	
Employment Law Made E-Z	G312		$14.95	
Collecting Child Support Made E-Z	G315		$14.95	
Limited Liability Companies Made E-Z	G316		$14.95	
Partnerships Made E-Z	G318		$14.95	
Solving IRS Problems Made E-Z	G319		$14.95	
Asset Protection Made E-Z	G320		$14.95	
Buying/Selling A Business Made E-Z	G321		$14.95	
Financing Your Business Made E-Z	G322		$14.95	
Profitable Mail Order Made E-Z	G323		$14.95	
Selling On The Web Made E-Z	G324		$14.95	
SBA Loans Made E-Z	G325		$14.95	
Solving Business Problems Made E-Z	G326		$14.95	
Advertising Your Business Made E-Z	G327		$14.95	
Shoestring Investing Made E-Z	G330		$14.95	
Stock Market Investing Made E-Z	G331		$14.95	
Fund Raising Made E-Z	G332		$14.95	
Money For College Made E-Z	G334		$14.95	
Marketing Your Small Business Made E-Z	G335		$14.95	

‡ *Prices are for a single item, and are subject to change without notice.*

continued on next page

	ITEM #	QTY.	PRICE‡	EXTENSION
Owning A No-Cash-Down Business Made E-Z	G336		$14.95	
Offshore Investing Made E-Z	G337		$14.95	
Multi-level Marketing Made E-Z	G338		$14.95	
Get Out Of Debt Made E-Z	G340		$14.95	
Your Profitable Home Business Made E-Z	G341		$14.95	
Winning Business Plans Made E-Z	G342		$14.95	
Mutual Fund Investing Made E-Z	G343		$14.95	
Business Startups Made E-Z	G344		$14.95	
Successful Resumes Made E-Z	G346		$14.95	
Free Stuff For Everyone Made E-Z	G347		$14.95	
Sub-total for Guides			$	

Made E-Z Kits

Bankruptcy Kit	K300		$24.95	
Incorporation Kit	K301		$24.95	
Divorce Kit	K302		$24.95	
Credit Repair Kit	K303		$24.95	
Living Trust Kit	K305		$24.95	
Living Will Kit	K306		$24.95	
Last Will & Testament Kit	K307		$19.95	
Buying and Selling Your Home Kit	K311		$24.95	
Employment Law Kit	K312		$24.95	
Limited Liability Company Kit	K316		$24.95	
Business Startups Kit	K320		$24.95	
Small Business/Home Business Kit	K321		$24.95	
Sub-total for Kits			$	

Made E-Z Books

Everyday Legal Forms & Agreements Made E-Z	BK407		$24.95	
Personnel Forms Made E-Z	BK408		$24.95	
Collecting Unpaid Bills Made E-Z	BK409		$24.95	
Corporate Records Made E-Z	BK410		$24.95	
Everyday Law Made E-Z	BK411		$24.95	
Vital Records Made E-Z	BK412		$24.95	
Business Forms Made E-Z	BK414		$24.95	
Sub-total for Books			$	

Labor Law Posters

☆ Federal Labor Law	LP001		$14.95	
☆ State Specific Labor Law see state listings below			$39.95	

State	Item#	QTY	State	Item#	QTY	State	Item#	QTY
AL	83801		KY	83817		ND	83834	
AK	83802		LA	83818		OH	83835	
AZ	83803		ME	83819		OK	83836	
AR	83804		MD	83820		OR	83837	
CA	83805		MA	83821		PA	83838	
CO	83806		MI	83822		RI	83839	
CT	83807		MN	83823		SC	83840	
DE	83808		MS	83824		S. Dakota not available		
DC	83848		MO	83825		TN	83842	
FL	83809		MT	83826		TX	83843	
GA	83810		NE	83827		UT	83844	
HI	83811		NV	83828		VT	83845	
ID	83812		NH	83829		VA	83846	
IL	83813		NJ	83830		WA	83847	
IN	83814		NM	83831		WV	83849	
IO	83815		NY	83832		WI	83850	
KS	83816		NC	83833		WY	83851	

☆ Required by Federal & State Laws

Sub-total for Posters			$	
TOTAL FOR ALL PRODUCTS			$	
Add Shipping & Handling $3.50 for first item, $1.50 for each additional item			$	
TOTAL PRODUCTS and S & H			$	
Florida Residents add 6% sales tax			$	
TOTAL OF ORDER			$	

‡ *Prices are for a single item, and are subject to change without notice.*

❋ **FOR FASTER SERVICE** ❋

Order by phone:
(954) 480-8933

Order by fax:
(954) 480-8906

SS 2001 r3

Name

Company

Position

Address

City

State   Zip

Phone
(   )

PAYMENT

❏ check enclosed, payable to:

Made E-Z Products, Inc.
384 S. Military Trail
Deerfield Beach, FL 33442

❏ charge my credit card: ❏ MasterCard ❏ VISA

ACCOUNT NO.   EXP. DATE

Signature: _____ (required for credit card purchases)

Index